In Between Days

Days

A Memoir of Heartbreak, Travel,
Films and the Search for Meaning

Luciana Colleoni

BALBOA.
PRESS

A DIVISION OF HAY HOUSE

Balboa Press books may be ordered through booksellers or by contacting:

Balboa Press
A Division of Hay House
1663 Liberty Drive
Bloomington, IN 47403
www.balboapress.com
1 (877) 407-4847

Because of the dynamic nature of the Internet, any web addresses or links contained in this book may have changed since publication and may no longer be valid. The views expressed in this work are solely those of the author and do not necessarily reflect the views of the publisher, and the publisher hereby disclaims any responsibility for them.

The author of this book does not dispense medical advice or prescribe the use of any technique as a form of treatment for physical, emotional, or medical problems without the advice of a physician, either directly or indirectly. The intent of the author is only to offer information of a general nature to help you in your quest for emotional and spiritual well-being. In the event you use any of the information in this book for yourself, which is your constitutional right, the author and the publisher assume no responsibility for your actions.

Any people depicted in stock imagery provided by Getty Images are models, and such images are being used for illustrative purposes only.
Certain stock imagery © Getty Images.

This book is a work of non-fiction. Unless otherwise noted, the author and the publisher make no explicit guarantees as to the accuracy of the information contained in this book and in some cases, names of people and places have been altered to protect their privacy.

Print information available on the last page.

ISBN: 978-1-9822-2709-8 (sc)
ISBN: 978-1-9822-2708-1 (e)

Balboa Press rev. date: 05/03/2019

Contents

Preface ix

Chapter 1   On childhood 1

Chapter 2   On teen age 40

Chapter 3   On being a young adult 92

Chapter 4   On starting life in England.......................... 120

Afterword.. 161

What's past is prologue.
- *William Shakespeare*

Preface

When I was a child I always thought I was going to be a writer. My mother would tell me stories of how, barely a baby, I would spend hours looking at books, comics, anything anyone left lying around. But I wouldn't just look at them, I would turn them slowly around and try to voice what I saw in baby speak. I can't remember whether I was in awe of words or pictures. As I got older, most family members knew to always give me books or stories as presents. Me and my sister Cristina were given a collection of fairy tales, I think it was 12 books in total, with illustrations which were actually photos of puppets beautifully dressed within a whole "film set". Cristina didn't much care for reading back then so I would have the whole collection to myself, and the pictures especially fascinated me, as some of them were 3D. I still don't understand how they managed to convey the fire at the witch's cabin in Hansel and Gretel. And as I grew up I kept encountering books which sent me straight into a parallel universe: The Little House on The Prairie series, Little Women, and Monteiro Lobato[1]'s entire body of work

At the age of fourteen I took it upon myself to write a letter to one of the most famous Brazilian poets, Carlos Drummond de Andrade, asking him for advice on how to become a writer – and a poet. I was probably still quite serious about it then. I didn't expect a reply, and I cannot remember what I said in my letter, but a reply was what I got, and it was quite an affectionate boost to my nascent inclination; his first words were: "Dear Luciana, I have with me your good letter...". I still have his letter as a sort of talisman. In it, he also talked about the need for reading, and reading some more, and then writing, and writing even more.

When I moved to London 23 years ago, and even before, I'd left writing behind, fascinated as I was – and still am – by filmmaking. I became really good at editing screenplays and helping shape the final text

---

[1] Famous Brazilian children's author, active around 1930s-1940s

for screenplays written by others. But part of me had shut down my early yearnings, even if I did write the screenplays for my first 2 short films. But in my mind they didn't look like the scripts most people write, and because they didn't really fit in perhaps my desire was just a flash in a pan. So, I decided to work with writers and collaborate instead of doing it myself.

I realised a while ago that what this decision concealed was, basically, fear. That I couldn't write as well as the people I'd been working with. Fear that, because English is not my first language, how can I express my deepest thoughts properly? And now I keep thinking about Joseph Conrad, a Polish immigrant to London in the late 19th century, who wrote some of the best-known novels in English literature: Heart of Darkness and Nostromo. Like me, Conrad arrived in England as an adult. Unlike me, he spoke little English and wasn't even a writer to start with. So, I have *some* advantage over him. But I mention him as an inspiration, because language should not be a barrier to a soul that longs to connect with others.

My last hurdle to start writing was: who would want to read a memoir by an unknown immigrant? And why, exactly, a memoir? Who would benefit from reading this? Who is my audience? The answer is, I don't know. I hope that my words can inspire someone in the pursuit of their dreams. I suspect that I will write this book in a somewhat random manner, as a stream of consciousness, describing my quest for spiritual omniscience and the fulfilment of my dreams with some seriousness but also a lot of humour.

I hope you enjoy it. I know I'll enjoy writing it as if I was drinking a long slow glass of water after a lifetime of thirst.

London, November 2018

ON CHILDHOOD

My mother says that when I was born all the *ypês*[2] were in bloom, full of yellow flowers. I've always assumed she says that to illustrate how much happiness my arrival caused in the family, and especially in her life. I have a very special and strong relationship with my mother and that may be why I always remember the things she says. I was the youngest. My sister Cris (short for Cristina) is almost 2 years older than me, and naturally wasn't as keen as everyone else when I claimed my baby place in the family. She threw a tin of talc on my head, which was definite evidence of her mood. Later as we grew up I looked up to her because she seemed to do all the things I lacked the guts or inclination for: smoke outside school, defy authority, date bad boys, run away from home, and a few more events I will describe later on.

But I'm getting ahead of myself; there's a little voice in my head telling me to rush past this section because it can't really interest anyone but myself or people who know me. But I wanted to write this book to examine my trajectory in life, how it has led me to where I am right now, the yearnings I've had over the years and how some of those could have been planted in early childhood. That's when the stage lights fall on parentage.

My father was a navy officer stationed in Rio de Janeiro when he married my mother, who was a composer & pianist from a well-to-do immigrant family in São José. Our stock is mostly Italian and Portuguese,

---

[2] Brazilian native tree with different colour flowers.

with a dash of Swiss, Syrian, Scottish and, I suspect, an ancient native Indian ancestor somewhere. After they got married, my parents went off to Europe on honeymoon, and returned to a very small apartment at the top of a hill in the Flamengo neighbourhood in Rio, which my mother soon strongly resented. I remember nothing from this period; we were both born in São José because my mother wanted to be near her parents for both births. The other reason for this is that my father was put on high alert in the fraught political and social upheaval in mid 60s Brazil. Not long after I was born there was a military coup which changed the social landscape for many years to come. But still that didn't affect us much – we lived in Rio for the first 3 or 4 years of my life, and what did affect us is what happened as we were about to move back to São José. It was February and we were staying with my grandparents. This was the end of summer and the season of heavy rains. My father was supposed to go back to Rio to start packing our home, but he could not travel as the roads had been blocked by floods. I think it was the next day when my mother heard on the radio that a building in Rio had collapsed, knocked down by big rocks rolling down the mountains just above. The radio report mentioned the address where it'd happened, and she realised it was our home in Rio. I was too young to remember the impact on my parents, but I know they were deeply shocked. We lost everything, all our possessions and, tragically, most of our friends and neighbours. I always heard this story as time passed, so I built a picture in my mind of the most graphic details. There were survivors. My father went back there to see if he could salvage anything, but it was all submerged in a pile of rubble and mud. We had to start from scratch.

We spent some time at my maternal grandmother's house, which to me was like some sort of fairy land which I will no doubt mention many times in this memoir. The house had to be sold some years ago because no one could afford to keep it, and no one wanted to live there either. But I still dream about it, about its vast empty rooms, its many gardens, where my grandmother Helena was the absolute ruler and creator. I remember her speaking to plants as she watered them, almost every day. Her back garden had sugar cane, camellias, pomegranates, avocado, lemons and coffee. The front porch as we walked in had a white jasmine tree, which scent lingered on even as we closed the front door. I've never forgotten the Easter egg hunts she organised. There were 6 of us kids, let loose in that gentle jungle to extract the treasures which *Vovó*[3] had so lovingly spread – and it was a massive and slick production: she covered each egg or treat with especially designed crochet covers aimed at the recipient. And once we'd retreated back in with our haul, someone would say: "Are you sure that's all there is?". Cue a renewed race to the garden in search of any missed goodies.

It was also in that magical garden, and around the age of 3, that I gained my first childhood memory laced with trauma: we were probably running around with cousins, like kids do, and I had started developing the habit of following my sister everywhere. I don't recall the circumstances and neither does anyone else who was an adult at the time (so much for memory!). But I have, imprinted in my mind, the picture of my sister and eldest cousin shutting a glass door to the greenhouse on me. Well, not just shutting it but actively pushing it against me and my little mid finger, which got stuck on the door frame. The result was a trip to A&E with my mother, where the doctor had some trouble finding a way to reattach the tip to the rest of my tiny finger. The funny thing is, if I look at the scar now and if I compare my left finger to the geography of the house and the door, it doesn't make sense – if anything it would have been the right finger. So how did this freeze frame get constructed in my toddler mind?

But I guess I can digress on this now, decades later. The psychological impact was likely to be something like "You're not wanted" in flashing neon lights. The picture in my mind is not a moving picture, but a still photograph. If I think of other, later events, the memory is more likely to be a short film. I guess my brain was not developed enough to shoot a little film of my own pain – which I don't recall at all - at the age of three! It's the wisdom of human beings that we cannot remember pain, physical or emotional, otherwise we would live in a permanent state of fear of moving ahead in life, taking chances, jumping into the unknown.

One of my other early memories is as follows: I'm about 5 years old, my mother is driving me to school, and I notice a homeless family sat on a street corner. I say to my mother: "A car should come, run them over and end this". Now, I don't remember the event or even saying those words, but I know them so well because I was told about it many times. My mother tried to gloss over what I'd said, as if to say poverty was a sight that bothered adults and I was only saying what they might be thinking.

---

[3] Grandma in Portuguese

But at the time she was shocked enough to gently tell me off and give me an education in compassion. As I said, I don't remember any of this, but the event became a famous story in our family: they were clearly raising a little monster, and this was told in jest and joke at various family events.

I have felt a profound impact from an event I don't even remember. I do remember the shame and the danger of really saying what's on my mind. Maybe it was to do with the fear of losing the love of those I cared about. But deeper down it was the fear that I might in fact be a "little monster" and so I began a practice of being quiet and rehearsing everything I had to say, just in case I was found out. Decades later and after many personal development courses and training, I am coming to terms with the fact that we all have a Shadow, and I surely gave mine an airing at a very early age. It is very liberating to find out I'm not the only asshole in the world. But just to make sure I'm not misunderstood - I obviously believe in equality of rights and justice for every human being and living creature on this earth. Damn, I even think inanimate objects deserve respect. I remember when an old chain of shops was going under in the UK, being sold for profit and the nearly 100-year-old business collapsing. I went into the Camden Town branch because it had huge CLOSING DOWN SALE signs. I wasn't particularly interested in bargains, but the appeal was that this shop would never again open its doors as its original name and there was something poignant about it. Trawling slowly through the aisles of sad merchandise and frantic people I had a distinct impression of a rape being committed. I know it's a charged word to be used in this context, but I can't find another to express the sense of a body or an entity being defiled. It is something I will come back to as this book progresses, especially in relation to films.

We had selected our favourite cousins since a very young age. Amélia was exactly one year younger than me, which means she was born on my birthday – well, her birthday as well. But when you're one and about to have your first birthday cake and everything gets postponed because there's a new baby arriving, it makes you wonder about the fairness of it all. As we got older, and whilst we lived in the same city, we would have our birthday parties combined. I can still remember our 6th birthday party, my cake was enormous, it had white icing with tiers and ribbons and flowers in yellow and green, the colours of the Brazilian flag. Amélia's cake was the same, but with green and pink flowers. I thought hers was prettier, but it was too late to change ownership. In the heat of the afternoon, with throngs of children mad with excitement and Coca-Cola, I soon forgot how much I disliked my cake's colours once it was sat inside a full tummy.

Amélia and her family lived upstairs from us, in a building which belonged to my grandad Armando, the last scion of a prestigious Italian family from inland São Paulo state. Her mum, aunt Odile, was an architect also married to an architect, my uncle Wilson. Their eldest son Raphael was also the eldest of us kids, the only boy and someone we absolutely looked up to. He was very clever, funny, and had us 3 wrapped around his little finger. He was also very bossy. Somehow, he always managed to get us to use our allowance to get him extra sweets, and at the same time feel incredibly honoured to do so. Children don't change very much – he's still like that now, almost 50 years later. Their parents were living near us because they needed a place to live while building their own home, which they also designed. Once the house was almost ready, they took us all to see it, and it looked like some sort of science fiction film set, something out of Kubrick's "2001": the main living room had a giant trap door that opened up like a submarine shaft, with a circular stair leading down to the study on the lower level. The whole house had 4 levels: the top was a solarium with a small pool, the street level was the main living area, the area below was the study, maids' quarters and garage, and downstairs was a play area with 2 massive blackboards with pots of chalk for the kids to draw. What united all floors was a cylinder-shaped tower staircase. Later on, they built a hollow area for a swimming pool, as the solarium was a bit dangerous for us kids. On their first day living there we celebrated with a meal cooked in their new kitchen, which was basically fried eggs with *Guarana* soft drinks. We loved it, of course.

We had other cousins but were never very close to them. I think it has to do with the experience of growing up together – Amélia and Raphael were the ones most similar in age to us. And the other cousins were from my father's side, and I wasn't so keen on my paternal grandmother. She had clear favourites and I wasn't one of them; my sister was, although she wasn't so keen on this grandma either. Edith was a rather quirky woman, very bossy and with a terrible temper. But she could be very funny, which I learned to appreciate as I got older, once I dropped the grudge I held for not being favourite material. She was originally from Rio de Janeiro, which means she had a raspy accent like all *cariocas*[4] do. She was also a mean cook, but the polar opposite in style, tidiness and dress sense to my maternal grandmother Helena. They had a polite 'vendetta' going on, likely to privately bet on whose household my parents would choose to spend Christmas Eve at. Because December 24th was the real celebration day in Brazil, sometimes followed by Midnight Mass. Dinner at grandmother Helena's was something I won't ever forget. She always set the same Christmas tree, a very old artificial white tree with ancient trinkets hanging from it and presents laid at its feet. Us kids could barely contain our excitement, but we still had to wait for dessert before opening them. Not that it was a hard task: the menu was the same every year, but it was exquisite: pork loin with her special sauce, rice and raisins, turkey and farofa (cassava flour) cooked with pork fat. Dessert was plum pudding. Now that I think about it, it sounds a bit Dickensian, but I've not tasted anything like it in my 23 years in Britain. Christmas Day was for leftovers (which were plenty) and visits to extended family. But even on the main date I remember my grandmothers' maids (she had 2) taking part in serving and having their own party in the lunch room. I'll have to explain the geography of the house: main events were held at the dining room, which had 2 sitting rooms and a hall next to it. That's where the family stayed.

I guess I'd probably have to explain the contractual realities of maids and cleaners in Brazil up to the 1990s – but I could be wrong on details so I'm sure someone will put me right once this book comes out. I don't presume to know exactly how things were everywhere, but since these are my memoirs I can relate my experience of it. All of my family members always had maids - us included. It seemed to be a given. My grandmother Helena had a cooker and a cleaner, even if she did most of the work herself or alongside them. Her massive house had a basement with many rooms, three of which were used by house maids at different times. While it is generally true that most maids in Brazil were people of colour, I don't think that was the case at either of my grandmother's houses. In fact, my aunt had a maid from Portugal, which was a statistical oddity. In terms of work/ leisure boundaries, it was an ill-defined sort of relationship; girls/women working as maids usually came to the big cities from the

---

[4] People born in Rio.

countryside, and they mostly lived with the families they worked for. Every apartment design in Brazil included maid's quarters, up to very recently. But they didn't have their own kitchen so in their downtime they obviously used the family kitchen, but curiously I cannot recall how that worked in practice. I guess mostly they went back home on weekends or kept so busy we never saw them. Myself and my sister had a maid/ nanny from Bahia, the north of Brazil, between the ages of 3 and 8. Her name was Eunice and she was a blast. When my mother left us for 4 months for a Music and Anthropology scholarship in Portugal, Eunice looked after us, along with my dad and grandmother Helena, who had a crafts shop next to our building. When Eunice got married we were her flower girls. My mother became godmother to her firstborn. And whenever I return to Brazil she always visits. I don't remember how well defined her contractual obligations were, but it naturally evolved in an organic way. But that is not always the case because there is a class system in place which makes it not such a simple exchange of services. At my grandmother's Christmas dinner, she always made sure there was a celebration in place for the maids. But they wouldn't share in ours, which strikes me as odd since my grandmother was from humble origins and a definite socialist soul. So, it has to be down to social structures.

When I was 8 years old, we were enrolled in a school, run by American nuns, where my mum was the music teacher. It had an amazing sense of freedom and I certainly don't recall any specific religious allegiance. I think the nuns were very forward thinking and some of them were pretty good at tap dancing. They had events such as Colour Day, in which parents had to bring food and drink only in primary colours (red, blue or yellow), and the Giant Cheese challenge, which is self-explanatory. The school was in the middle of a forest and the classrooms were like a Scandinavian summer camp, with massive chalk boards and big glass windows facing woodland. Girls' uniforms were plain dresses of one colour for each child, so at break time the place heaved like a snaking rainbow. I had blue dresses for summer, and red dresses for winter. I really loved that school. And yet I can recall the social structures present. There was a girl in my class called Julia, the school cleaner's daughter. I can remember her sitting not far from me, in her orange dress, rocking awkwardly in her chair. Julia was shunned by others because she was on a scholarship; she had free tuition because of her mum. I didn't know what to make of her, but like the other kids I avoided her. There seemed to be a silent agreement between us that to hang out with Julia would risk 'loser' contagion…and so we didn't. I don't think anyone was cruel or bullied her but thinking about it all those years later I can almost see it in her face, that she knew what was going on. And months later it was probably her mum who had to hose me down in the school yard when I pooed my pants just before a PE lesson. I learned something about humiliation that day, standing in the laundry sink as the possible result of diarrhoea trickled down my legs. Decades later I still have a clear image of that day, and I wonder what sorts of images Julia would have kept in her mind as well.

We left São José one year later, on another of my dad's naval postings. We were sent to the north of Brazil, a state called Bahia. Our new home was to be at the military base of Itambé, just 20 mins outside Porto Seguro. There was quite a bit of adjustment needed for the first few months there. The naval base was idyllic, and we had one of the houses right opposite the beach, a tropical paradise with palm trees and white sand, with sun all year round. We were surrounded by other navy officers and their families, most of them with kids our age or a bit older, and we had no trouble forming gangs pretty much straight away – well I usually let my sister take the lead whilst I tagged along, which sometimes worked, but other times backfired. Especially during our teenage years. But at this time, it was pure innocent childhood where all (it seemed) were welcome.

We were enrolled at Escola do Futuro which translates as 'school of the future'. There was nothing futuristic about it, in fact it was housed in a grandiose turn of the century palace, and the teaching methods were pretty ancient as well. Quite a shock compared to the tap-dancing nuns. At Escola do Futuro we had old teachers, who looked ancient even if they probably weren't that old. There was a venerable old teacher who sat on an armchair at the entrance, and every student had to kiss her on the cheek every morning. She was small and fat and looked like a cross between a frog and a sphinx. I remember her cheek was cold and flabby like a pillow with no feathers. But we had to do it, and she never smiled or said anything, she just sat there as a procession of slightly cowed children formed a line to kiss her. In my own class I had a teacher who called herself Grandma Ondina– and insisted we did the same. She was proper old, and quite cruel. She would hit kids with a (thankfully) plastic ruler if they proved to be dim or slow. Which meant that her usual targets were twins Alberto and Eriberto, two scrawny boys who appeared to be both dim AND slow. It was either the ruler or a slight push on the shoulder if she was feeling charitable, which I got on a couple of occasions. We also had cards given out to us every morning with the Morning Prayer, which we had to say out loud in group at the start of every lesson. And at the end of our year with Grandma Ondina we were all given our own copy of the Morning Prayer. On my copy she had written a personal dedication saying that she hoped I'd think of her every time I said my prayers. But I realised she'd written the same message on all copies, even the poor twins got the same. I didn't really stop to think too much about whether I was outraged or entertained by her or the school. I know that I mocked the entire institution relentlessly to my parents, but I must have done it so well they were in turn highly entertained by my depictions of teachers, and also the way they spoke – *Baianos*[5] had quite a pronounced accent and quite different from the white South we came from. It was (and is) a predominantly black state, perhaps due to slave trade arriving there and also northwards, directly from Africa, up until the 19th century. Outside the school gates there were a couple of big *baiana* sellers of acarajé, a local snacky dish made of beans and prawns with spicy sauce. They looked amazing, all dressed in white lace, turbans and bling, sat around white cloths, with a pot of boiling oil of *dendê*[6] where they fried bean cakes, cut them open and filled them with prawn or fish stew. I suspect we were too young to try it, even if the local kids who also went to our school seemed to have no problem eating it.

Escola do Futuro was right in the centre of town and we had to be driven on the Navy school bus every morning. I remember the first time we ever got on that bus, we'd just arrived, and it was likely our first day at school, no uniforms yet. We didn't want to go to school and decided to stage a protest. Well - I let my sister stage the protest and I'd see how that would go, to be precise. It didn't go well at all. My father dispatched my sister into the bus with a smack on the bottom and I knew I should follow closely behind to avoid any further embarrassment. My sister was into sedition whereas I was more politically minded, from an early age it

---

[5] Born in Bahia.
[6] Palm oil.

seems. But it didn't take very long for us both to blissfully adapt to life in this strange and unexpected part of our country. Our daily drive to school was always entertaining, because we used to drive past scenes I had never witnessed before. The areas around the Naval base were mostly very deprived, and yet looking out of the window every day it didn't strike me as a miserable place. We'd see kids our age dressed in rags run around shacks built all along rickety bridges of bamboo, playing and jumping into lakes of dark polluted water. I say polluted in hindsight, because at the time all I knew was that those kids seemed to be having more fun than me, on my way to Grandma Ondina. But even so, at the age of 8 I could tell this was no place to live: the air was fetid. One day we drove past a dead donkey by the side of the road. Every day, for the next fortnight, we were fascinated to watch how the animal decomposed little by little, until all was left was its carcass, because nobody bothered to move it. It was a better biology lesson than anything Escola do Futuro could teach us.

Outside school hours we didn't really spend much time in the city. We had too much fun back at Itambé, because there was a world of play available there. We didn't much care about the beach, except when the tide change brought lots of dead jellyfish on to the sand. They were small, the size of a tea plate, and no longer harmful when dead. They had a beautiful 3D like mandala in their centre. The texture was like gelatine, and you could slice them like a flan, so we would play market owners and restaurants. Low tide also brought a high number of small dead fish to the shore, so our market supply was complete. We hung out with maybe 4 other kids who lived close by, and my sister also got the neighbours' dogs involved. The house to our left was taken by a friend of my dad's, Captain Fausto, who had a wife, 3 sons and a collie dog named Argos. The house to our right was Captain Neves', who had 2 kids, no wife and 2 dogs, a poodle named Veruska and a Weimaraner called Fizz. Argos and Fizz would follow my sister everywhere, despite their owners' objections, so they became part of our 'gang'. We'd roam the streets freely, on our bikes, like a scene out of ET, finding the next weird thing where we'd least expect. We did find a dead man on the beach once – or rather, the others found it before I did. I remember just looking at the scene from afar and being aware of someone lying very still and not moving. Later I learned it was a dead person. I didn't understand much about death or life at this stage, but I definitely understood death from that moment on: it meant you will never move ever again, and your colour will also change. But there was no dread or fear associated with that realisation. I guess we were too busy having fun.

On certain afternoons, there was a baby blue VW camper van driving around the base, announcing its wares: it was the baker's van, and as we could all smell the fresh donuts on its trunk, we all rushed home as we heard the badly regulated engine spluttering around the corner. We would crowd around the back of the van, eager to get our hands on custard goodies, at the same time that my dad arrived from work on his jeep, so the timing was near perfect. My mother kept herself busy doing all sorts of courses in town, mostly to do with thorny subjects like Musicology and Pataphysics. Being a Navy wife, she had to park her career to one side and follow my dad on his various postings. She didn't actually have to do that, given that Captain Neves next door didn't have his kids' mother living there, but we were lucky that she chose family over career, which is a choice I have learned to thank her for over the years, because she chose to raise us. And I don't know why, but in Bahia I developed an intense attachment to my mother. During my first days at Escola do Futuro she had to stay with me, or I would panic if she wasn't there. And I wasn't a toddler – I was 8 years old. This lasted throughout my adolescence, and it was an attachment which I hid like a dirty secret, like it was shameful not to go to sleepovers because I missed mum. I haven't really thought about this for many years as it eventually faded away. Well, I moved abroad after all.

During our time in Bahia it turns out that one of my dad's duties was to choose the films to be shown at the base's cinema. It must have been a rotation system with other officers to keep a 'balanced' programme, so every second weekend a roll of film posters would arrive at our home, and I looked forward to the unfurling of garish colours across our front room. We didn't have a say on what my dad picked but over the years I've noticed he has impeccable taste and is a film lover. The local cinema was my first real connection with film as it is meant to be seen, in a dark temple, in communion with other people. There are films I saw there for the first time which I never forgot. I once heard my mum had gone to the cinema and I wanted to surprise her. So, I went there with a couple of friends, after dinner. There were no charges and no restrictions on age (I doubt this would happen anywhere today), and we had no idea which film was playing. I found a seat right behind my mum and sat there quietly, whispering to my friends how I was going to suddenly appear to her side and scare her. But I didn't, because what happened was that the images on the screen started to slowly hypnotize me. I found myself mesmerized by what I was watching: it was a film set in the early 1900s, with haunting music, and there were images of a blonde boy on a beach and a sad older man watching him from a deck chair. The sadness of the old man seemed to follow a crescendo with the music, and some of his hair was painted because a drop of hair colour rolled down his cheek at the end, like a black tear. I didn't know what I'd seen, but I was so engrossed by the experience I only snapped out of it when my mum grabbed my shoulders as the lights went on. Years later I learned the film was called *Death in Venice*, by an Italian director called Lucchino Visconti. I also saw Nicholas Ray's *55 Days in Peking* at that cinema. But I only discovered the titles many years later, because they burned such an indelible memory in my retina at the age of 9 that I had to find out what I'd seen.

The other very unusual and interesting fact about this cinema is that it was a cinema only Monday to Saturday. On Sundays it doubled up as a church. There were no significant changes to the decorations or any nod to Catholic worship, except from a lectern placed at the front. Mass was led by Chaplain Almeida, a kindly man who couldn't really keep the kids in check. Sometimes I'd see some of the older kids who'd already had first communion go back to their seats after being given the holy wafer and look very introspective with their eyes closed. I became very curious about what the whole rite entailed. Some of us tried to break into Chaplain Almeida's wafer cupboard after mass to try and nick some and see what all the fuss was about, but we made too much noise and had to flee. My mother had already asked me and my sister if we'd like to have our first communion soon. I wasn't particularly interested in mass or religion, but I wasn't NOT interested either. I wanted to know why people looked so intense after communion and was certain it was all about the wafer. So, I said yes, even after mum telling us how much of an important commitment it was and how we'd need to attend mass regularly if we took this step...

The date was set for December, high summer, and we both got new lace white dresses and special candles with red velvet ribbon around them.

There were about 6 other kids having their first communion on the same date. We got prayer cards with all our names printed on them, to give away as mementos. When the time came for my first actual communion and the wafer was placed in my mouth, I more or less did what I'd seen the older kids doing: walk back pensively to my chair, close my eyes and wait for the amazing revelation which was certainly just around the corner. The only thing I was aware of was the staleness of the wafer and how it stuck to the tongue, the fact it tasted like my least favourite biscuit and the absolute absence of any mystery. But my one overriding memory from that day was the wonderment of Chaplain Almeida preaching the word of Jesus Christ and God against the backdrop of a white cinema screen. It was in the blink of an eye that my vocation in the world came to pass. Perhaps this was the mystery I had longed for, although this was not apparent for many years.

After the religious celebration, a feast of sorts had been set up at the opposite end of the beach, where a big straw hut hosted most community parties. Charged with the excitement of youth and having forgotten the wafer disappointment, I set about joining the others in running and awaiting the time we'd be allowed to eat the sweets on show. Official permission from the adults was taking ages to come forth, partly because they seemed perfectly happy to chat and drink wine, so one of the naughtier kids asked Chaplain Almeida if we were allowed to go for the sweets. But he asked in a lower voice, knowing full well the poor Chaplain was part deaf. This kid – his name escapes me – asked "Father, can we throw sweets?", to which the Chaplain, thinking the question was whether we could EAT the sweets. answered 'Of course my son'. What followed was a slapstick scene, with us partly stuffing ourselves with sugar and partly engaging in an epic sweet throwing battle. The parents and adults were likely a bit drunk by now, but not enough to try and stop it and find out how it had started. The poor Chaplain sat on a chair, looking very confused as a volley of chocolate bonbons flew past his nose.

The Americans.

That's what we called the American family who came to live at the Naval base. They were immediately an object of extreme interest to all of us kids. The only notion of anything American to me previously was that one of the other Navy officers had also been posted to the US for a couple of years, and his daughter Patty had all these amazing Barbie and

Ken dolls with their houses with fake drawn pools. She was extremely possessive of her toys, but we were allowed to watch her play with them. American Barbie dolls were very different from their Brazilian alternative, Susi, a slightly gaze-into-the-void doll which had none of the glossy hair or Malibu accoutrements that went with Barbie. Susi's "boyfriend" was another frozen looking doll called Beto. They were perfectly fine toys to play with, until we discovered the world of Barbie and American toys. Which we could not get anywhere except the US. But the American family, the McAllisters, were a good substitute for our endless curiosity. At first, we visited their new home with our parents. I immediately sensed this was not a home like any other; it *smelled* different. As I got older and came into contact with other American navy families abroad, I realised they brought EVERYTHING from America with them, even food. And the McAllisters also had piles of *Pringles* potato crisps on endless supply, boxes of the stuff in their garage. To me they tasted a bit synthetic - but fascinating. They had 3 kids: the eldest, Mary, was around my age. The middle child was Beth, and the youngest was Sean. We became play friends, and I'm not entirely sure how we communicated, because they didn't speak Portuguese and I didn't speak English. Beth would sometimes talk to me like we were old friends, and I remember looking at her and thinking, 'I have no idea what you're saying'. Perhaps that is the reason we started learning English at about this time, with a private teacher. It must have been frustrating hanging out with those kids and understanding nothing they said. I don't think the McAllisters stayed in Bahia more than a year, but they gave me an idea about the world outside my immediate life, something I'd not considered before.

My sister started to rebel during our stay at Itambé. Her attempt at not going to school was the first definitive act I recall, but the writing was on the wall. I usually admired her initiative, because I was never going to follow suit. The school bus episode was enough warning. But I think in her mind she would never class as rebellion her attempts to assert herself in the world. She started going out with another officer's son, which didn't go down well with my dad. I guess he thought that she was too young to be thinking about dating boys at 10 years old. I definitely was, but that didn't stop the other kids concocting a rumour about my new boyfriend Pedro– a cute toothy boy with a fringe who was as clueless about romance as I was. But as a matter of fact, only 2 years earlier and whilst on holiday to my grandmother's beach house, me and my cousins had this challenge with the neighbour's kids, one of which was also supposed to be my 'boyfriend', whereby we would lower our pants and compare the different bits. But the attention span of 6-year olds is probably more to do with the intangible notion that there is something which differentiates boys and girls, and what can that be? Admittedly we were likely goaded on by my eldest cousin Raphael, who was 10 at the time. He was the oracle and we would do whatever he asked us. The neighbour's daughter, Martha, a bit older than me, wore a kids' bikini which had a pointy fake bra. She was probably only 7, but that fake bra added a certain allure we found alien to childhood but at the same time a taste of mysteries to come. She looked proper grown up to me although she was probably just about 2 years older.

Our holidays at my paternal grandmother's beach house were idyllic. It was on the southern tip of the Northern coast of São Paulo state, almost opposite an island called Ilha Grande (big island). The small fishing village still bore witness to its colonial past, the two main churches built in the 17th century standing strong in the face of sea erosion and uncontrolled tourism. The house itself was small and quirky, but my grandmother had a knack for making it homely and cosy. It had been built in the 50s, when the whole region was mostly quiet and very few houses dotted the hills around the sea. One of my uncles, an architect, had designed the house in keeping with the landscape, so it was a simple bungalow with a couple of annexes built and a housekeeper's quarters at the entrance. I spent most summers there, between the ages of 5 and 12, by which time my aunt and uncle, the architect couple, had built their own home a bit further north. But this house had something special about it; we would arrive through a long driveway up to a massive mango tree which invariably dropped its produce on our car throughout the summer, leaving trails of soft yellow flesh on the roof and bonnet. My grandmother also raised hens and ducks, and they had a coop next to the housekeeper's bungalow. Next to the big mango tree was also a small courtyard where she grew ferns and climbers. As soon as we arrived, the first thing we'd do was to find the paths along the side of the house, shaded by hibiscus and coconut trees, and run across the rolling lawn that framed the sea. Bury our feet into the soft white sand and splash around on the shores of calm water, making our toes wriggle and grab lumps of wet sandy shells. On days of blazing sunshine, it was the generous shade of the almond tree that kept us cool and refreshed, along with jugs of fresh lemonade ferried from my grandmother's kitchen.

The actual configuration of the house defied logic. It had two small bedrooms (which I never understood as my grandparents had at least 2 kids when it was built), both of which faced the sea. The room we stayed in had 2 bunk beds made out of wood and painted sky blue, with white walls and sky-blue furniture. None of us liked sleeping under the top beds because we would often get dead insects or cockroaches dislodged from the wood panels falling on us during the night, as the person above moved in their sleep. On arrival there was always a dispute to determine who would get which bunk bed. But the white & blue room was also strangely calming, hypnotizing even. I loved slowly falling asleep listening to the roar of the sea just outside. Before slipping into bed I'd press my face against the mosquito net window to try and make out the shape of the sea through the darkness of the night as I tried to match sound and vision. And I don't ever remember seeing a moonlit night from that window.

The room had a smell of "age", of old things, that lingered long after we arrived. On the dresser there was always a bottle of faded rose perfume and a case of *Coty* pressed powder. I assumed they belonged to my grandmother but couldn't understand why someone old would need those things…She had personal belongings dotted around the house, no matter who would be staying at the time. My grandfather Raposo was a quiet man who didn't seem to have an active voice in how his family life was run. He would sit in his terrace chair, facing the sea, always reading. I barely remember the sound of his voice because he spoke so little. He was also hard of hearing which made it a considerable effort to hold any sort of conversation with him. By contrast, my grandmother had fingers on many social pies, so to speak – she knew all the neighbours and organized everything in the household, from soft furnishings to how food was prepared. The whole house was decorated to her taste, which was somewhat bizarre but also pretty intriguing. The floors of the main rooms were tiled, which was a practical move – people would come into the house with sandy feet and tiles were easier to clean. There were crochet hammocks hung from the main terrace, off limits to anyone wanting to relax and watch the sea with damp bathing suits. Next to the main living room there was a small rectangular shaped room that served no real purpose except to spook small kids like me: it was full of relics and artefacts collected over the years, African demon masks, old shells, woven tableaux and the indelible smell of old age. Later on, she managed to install a small TV there, but the reception wasn't great, and my dad would spend a long time battling with the aerial when my grandmother wanted to watch Silvio Santos, a dreadful Sunday TV variety show.

At the entrance to this room there was a mural painted by my aunt Odile. Before she could afford her own beach house, she would spend summers there with us, and as a thank you to my grandmother she painted a St Francis of Assisi surrounded by fish and birds. I don't know why she chose St Francis or whether it was a request, but it was a soothing picture. Years later when the house had to be sold, it was pointed out to the buyer how valuable my aunt's art had become, but eventually we learned that he bulldozed the entire house. It also came to pass, years later, that the clear emerald sea facing the house soon became too polluted for people to swim in, partly because the local village had become one of the points of oil commerce and exploration. And cruise ships stopping over on the way up north seemed to delight the local authorities for the business they brought, but the area suffered as a result. But by then we were much older and had our own holiday home, much further north in the wilder bit of coast.

Before that, we started to spend our summer holidays at my aunt's new beach home, at a calm bay enclave called White Beach (because of the colour of its sand) which seemed to be untouched by tourist developments. The first couple of years there were more basic, there was no fridge or electricity as the grid was not yet installed in those wild nature spots. But it was great fun. We used gas lamps at night, and they had a clay oven which was used to bake pizzas. No real entertainment at night, no TV or radio but we spent time doing puzzles or playing cards. Like my grandmother's place, this one also faced the sea. We'd get up early to enjoy the beach before the sun got too hot. The stretch of beach was quite small, even for a bay, and you could walk the whole length and back in over 20 minutes. At the end nearer to us there was a rocky stretch which we loved to explore, because you could actually cross over to the next bay beach through the rocks, but some of it was a bit dangerous for kids, even though we liked to pretend that wasn't the case. Some of the rocks were covered in moss and algae, which made them slippery. But it was a stunning adventure, slowly climbing up and finding water pools full of small fish and strange looking crabs, and colonies of black limpets breathing out bubbles as the high tide waves started to creep in. It was a tiring but exhilarating exercise. Other mornings when we didn't feel so brave we would just spend time in the sea, with floating lilos and a wooden canoe which was owned and managed by my eldest cousin Raphael, who operated a strict invitation-only policy. Us youngsters couldn't get on it, but we found other ways to amuse ourselves.

I don't know who started the cockle hunting race, but it soon reached fever pitch. Since we couldn't get on my cousin's canoe, we were persuaded by the adults to dig into the sand where the waves crashed and find cockles for lunch. I don't remember being that interested in sea food then, unless it was covered in bread crumbs and fried, but as a game it definitely proved a challenge: plastered with sun cream, and tired after splashing in the sea for most of the early morning, I placed my plastic bucket next to my 'work' area and dug my hands into the soft white sand, feeling the bubbles and pockets of water under my palms as the waves gently wrapped around my legs. Soon I realized that some bubbles were the point where I should dig for cockles. I would bring up handfuls of wet sand and rub them together until they revealed around 2 or 3 cockles in each bundle of sand. The first time I did this I was distracted by the amazing design of the shells, they were either light blue, grey or terracotta, but with almost the same pattern. They weren't shaped like shells or cockles, but more like small diamonds. I was engrossed in my task and so were the other kids – I don't think we viewed it as a competition, although we each brought a bucketful of the sea creatures home later. These were used to make what some people might now call a *paella,* but in those days, it was just called cockles rice. And it was delicious.

Cooking has been a tradition in my family since I was a kid. I grew up watching my grandmother Helena cook Italian, Lebanese and traditional Brazilian food. She was born in the temperate climate hills of Rio state, in a Swiss immigrant enclave. Her mother was Swiss, and her father was a Syrian immigrant who had previously become an American citizen and fought in the Spanish American war in 1898. I remember grandma Helena as one of the strongest women I ever met. She honoured her heritage partly with food, and a lot of it was Lebanese, but at the time of her father's birth, Beirut was part of Syria and there was no Lebanon. I only really understood how Swiss-oriented she was when I visited Zurich and Basel years later and saw so many surnames of family relations splashed across businesses and vans. We stopped at a small restaurant in Basel serving homemade food, and it felt like a jump back in time to grandma's kitchen. The meals were cooked by two middle aged Swiss women, and the whole place was spotless, just like her kitchen.

Not a lot of people know that there was a planned immigration scheme championed by the Portuguese king João VI for Swiss nationals to own and work plots of land in southern Brazil. He also wanted Swiss men to be recruited as his personal Swiss guard, much like in the Vatican. At this point it is worth mentioning that the Portuguese Royal family had escaped to Brazil just as the Napoleonic troops were entering Lisbon in the early 1800s. They settled court in Rio, and during their reign in the colony they built the National Library, Royal palaces and the Botanical Gardens. The king's son, Pedro, became the first Brazilian emperor around 1822, and kicked off Brazilian independence soon after (or before? I did learn this in school!). His son, Pedro II, was finally exiled in 1899 when the Republic was declared. But before this could happen there was wave after wave of immigrants arriving in Brazil, either seeking a better life or lured in by promises of land to work on and eventually own. The Swiss were eager to leave their cantons because a lot of them were either criminals, or orphans, or *heimatlos*(stateless) people – or just families hungry for opportunities not found in Europe. Germans started coming in the 1830s, mostly to the south of Brazil where the climate somewhat resembled the Fatherland. The Italian wave was much bigger and designed to replace slave labour in coffee plantations in the South, after the abolition in 1888. For them, it was about land and the recent political upheavals in Italy, with the unification of separate kingdoms in 1868 which had brought uncertainty and hunger. My grandad Armando's family arrived in the last decade of the 19th century. They were dirt poor, and his father Benedetto ferried trolleys of coal to help the family budget at the age of 10 (about the age I was digging cockles for fun). I always heard stories of what a harsh man he was, but single minded in his pursuit of success and wealth. Which he achieved, perhaps because he had seen the other side of comfort and abundance. He was a shrewd business man. He used to say to his sons: 'always seek to have

3 sources of wealth: coin, paper(stocks) and brick (property)'. My grandad didn't follow this through so well, as he was more of a dreamer. But his father sensed his talent and sent him back to Milan to study textile design: by then he had a silk fabric factory and they made their own silk ties so my grandfather became head designer after almost 3 years in Milan. Even as a grown up, hearing his stories of life in Milan in the 1920s, I couldn't help but feel amazed by his praising of Benito Mussolini and his social policies, which he must have seen and experienced first-hand. He couldn't believe that was the same Mussolini who allied himself with the Nazis. To him that must have been some dreadful mistake. He had a small wall bust of Mussolini which he kept in his office, and which my mum inherited, and which I will also likely inherit – the dilemma of what to do with it…she keeps it because it reminds her of her beloved father, as I might, for the same reason, but probably buried in a drawer like she has.

Italian food was the main fare because of my grandad Armando, who kept the Italian tradition going. My grandmother, although not Italian, was a fabulous cook, and incorporated all she learned from her mother in law at the Italian kitchens of the Colleonis. I don't remember my grandmother ever having a social life. She did own a gift shop in the late 60s/ early 70s which was her pride and joy. She sourced all the arts and crafts from around Brazilian regions, and travelled north by bus, on a 2-day journey, just to find local craftsmen to supply her shop. I think she loved being out and about with different people, and engaging in intelligent conversations, but the shop had to be shut down as the pressure of housework loomed. She was no feminist, even if she was at the peak of her female power…after that, she basically kept the kitchen going, and I'd often find her downstairs by the lower garden level where the laundry unit was, either washing or ironing. She had domestic help but was always working harder than anyone. The laundry was huge, it had two big tiled basins and an old 1940s washing machine which I used as a spa pool for my dolls. I loved spending time with her, listening to her old yarns of childhood spent in farms in Rio. She was the eldest of nine children and had to give up her education to help raise her brothers and sisters. I still wonder what brilliant things she might have achieved if she'd been able to graduate. She was a deeply interesting, spiritual woman, with more than a bit of a temper. She was very religious, steeped in Catholic upbringing from both parents. Every fortnight or so there would be a knock on her door and a small thin woman holding what looked like a tall doll house would come in and leave it with us for another fortnight. This was a 'reliquary', a sort of altar with doors opening outwards. Inside, it did look like a doll house, but more like something a bit serious was happening. Some stern looking angels and saints, statues made out of wood with some bits missing. My grandmother would choose the freshest white camellias from her garden, and place them in a gold rimmed jug, right in the centre of the altar. And so, this set piece would remain in the house for a good 15 days, until the same skinny old lady would come to collect it. I always thought it looked too big to be carried by someone so small, around the steep hills our street merged with.

My grandmother had lost a 6-year-old daughter to meningitis, many years before, probably in the 1940s. There was also a permanent altar to this child, called Carmen, on her main dresser. A couple of pictures of her in healthier times, dressed as a columbine for carnival, and on another smiling broadly for the camera. There was always a vase with fresh camellias on that dresser. At the time of Carmen's death my grandmother got pregnant with my uncle Saulo, which I can only imagine was the attempt to lift the veil of grief which must have descended over their household. Uncle Saulo's later story is also tinged with some strange coincidences and a whiff of the supernatural – but I'll touch on that later.

At the age of 11 I moved into their house, along with my mother and sister, whilst my dad worked in Rio during the week and visited us on weekends. We lived with them for 3 years, until my sister's looming teenage rebellion would clash directly with my grandmother's strict ways, causing my mum to look for somewhere else for us to lodge once their bickering became too much. But the time we spent there holds the most vivid memories in my mind. It was almost like a Hobbit household, each little corner holding its special mystery. Later, in my 20s, when I was in Art college nearby, I would often turn up at lunchtime because I knew I'd eat much better there than anywhere else in the neighbourhood. But I did especially enjoy finding my grandfather sat on his favourite rocking chair, in the dark and cool hallway, with its check black and white marble floor and the ominous but strangely soothing tick tack of the old wall clock. He never seemed surprised to see me, and I suspect he would have been immersed in his own private mind time travel just as I rang the doorbell. As I write this it hits me how much I miss him. I was too young when he passed away, unable to ask and probe into the deepest thoughts in his artistic mind.

But back to childhood and at the threshold of teen age, he wasn't always sitting in the hallway; we'd often find him in his office, building contraptions, inventing things and thinking word puzzles to amuse us with. It seems that people we love in our lives, the elders, are like foundations of a house being constructed, and we are this house. Once it's built we can't see the things that hold it together but they're there, invisible to the eye but nevertheless lovingly holding us. I dare say that is the case even in families where people dislike each other. My grandfather reminds me of an old and strong oak tree, but a funny one. He loved to joke, and he wasn't actually that funny, but he was unique. I once found him in my mother's old study meditating with a copper pyramid as a hat. This was probably pretty forward thinking and a bit weird back then. He wasn't exactly eccentric, but he had ideas I've never encountered since and he did build little machines no one had a clue what to do with. I think the death of his young daughter hit him very hard. Even 40 years later I don't recall him ever laughing out loud. He more or less ruled the household, but my grandmother was probably the actual boss, the decider of everything. Hmm. Much like with my paternal grandparents: women ruled. Grandma Helena spent the entire time cooking, sewing, cleaning or in the garden, talking to her plants. She must have taught a generation of young girls how to make pasta dough. She had a pasta machine permanently set on one of the marble work tops, because pasta was freshly made at least twice a week. It was the more traditional fare my grandfather favoured, like fettuccine, polenta and *cappelletti in brodo* which I always remember in fondness and comfort. It was like a chicken soup with meat dumplings wrapped in pasta. She also made the best gnocchi I ever tasted, until I tried it at our local Sardinian restaurant. Italian food is actually not that hard to make, but the trick is making it with love and soul. Knowledge helps as well. She learned from my great grandmother Teresina, a prime example of gargantuan Italian women, literally born cooking.

When we moved to their house, the elders decided that me and my sister would share a room. I don't know why they didn't split us because there was one extra room on the family floor upstairs. All the rooms in their house had different colours; ours was white, and it also used to be my grandmother's dressing room, which she gave up for us. I was glad they didn't put me in the extra room because its walls were dark pink, and it was full of old relics which I had a bit of a dislike about – much like at my paternal grandmother's beach house. We stayed in that little room for 3 years, with some of the furniture unmoved. We weren't allowed to play around the dresser, which had 3 mirrors and another mirrored panel on it, holding all sorts of porcelain little people and animals. It was off-limits to us; my sister couldn't care less as she was more interested in skate boards and boys, but I'd sit nearby fascinated by the silent game I imagined was going on between the painted figures. Sometimes I'd go sit at my grandfathers' study after school, watching him construct his machines or marvel at his old collection of Reader's Digest magazines. Other times I'd go into my mother's bedroom, which was mustard coloured, with an annex where she kept a piano, to hear her play her favourite pieces. A lot of the times I'd hang around the kitchen watching my grandmother and helpers prepare food for the week, or sometimes when there was a public holiday coming up they would be super busy with designing menus – well, choosing what to make sounds more accurate – and drawing up shopping lists. The pasta machine would be busy, and the entire lunch room table would be taken over by strips of drying pasta and raviolis or savoury pastry being assembled. I developed a taste for cooking by watching the goings on in that kitchen. I fancied myself their disciple, and once at the age of 11 I followed a magazine recipe for Christmas cookies. I followed it to the letter, except when I failed to notice that I'd rolled out my dough over a marble top recently cleaned with detergent. I only realised what had happened when they came out of the oven, smelling of soap and vanilla. It didn't deter me though. My next attempt was my aunt's easy peasy chocolate cake, but this time instead of sunflower oil I used extra virgin olive oil. My mother kindly had a slice or two, but my sister mocked me like only she knew how. By that stage she was also interested in cooking, but as a much more acute observer than me. She became a chef, specialising in vegetarian and vegan cooking - and she is a true magician with food. But at that time, because she had such a difficult relationship with my grandmother, I never expected her to be willing to learn from some annoying elder relative. I still carry the ethos of what grandma Helena's cooking was about, which my mother also followed. For pasta, one cup of flour plus one egg, and double it as required. Be thrifty, waste not, want not, but no economy when it comes to feeding people.

There were often homeless or hungry people ringing the bell asking for a plate of food. My grandma was always prepared for it, she kept cheap tin plates around and filled them with whatever we were having. And added a bread roll, which is something no Italian meal ever goes without. The plates were usually returned empty, left under her gate. And so, their routine went on, with some trepidations sometimes. I remember one time when a woman with two young children turned up out of nowhere. She claimed she'd had a relationship with my grandmother's tearaway nephew Marco and these kids were the result, and now they had nowhere to go. I don't think any evidence was produced, partly because the little boy was named Marco as well, and the little girl was a namesake for my grandma's late sister. Besides, they were both the spitting image of their dad. So, they stayed on for a bit, eventually finding other accommodation with help from extended family. My grandad was glad to see them go, as he had been glad to see so many of my grandmother's extended family leave after enjoying his hospitality. He never said a word, but it was obvious he didn't enjoy having his home taken over by people he considered strangers. My grandma suffered, though. She became attached to the little boy, and he to her. She had a gift for nurturing children without ever patronising or belittling them, and I experienced that first hand. We were the only grandchildren who ever lived with her and so we developed a very close bond. She could be a bit scary because she did have a temper, but she was brutally honest, and never mollycoddled us. And yet I could feel the deep love she had for us, how she guided us daily. Even my sister, who for a time probably hated her, now recognises what a profoundly positive presence she had been in our lives.

I notice how I keep going back to her in these pages. She was like a sturdy compass for my whole life, apart from my parents. At the time we lived with her my dad was effectively living in Rio during the week and would get the bus down to see us on weekends. That was quite a commitment. It was a 5-hour trip each way. I guess he really missed us, even if Rio was – still is - a real den of pleasure. He had a flat on the 3rd floor of a 1940s building in the heart of Ipanema, home of the famous tall and tanned and young and lovely girl. As a matter of fact, there were a lot more of those all over Rio, as my mum well knew. We spent a few days there on a school holiday, hanging out with my friend Denise, another Navy kid. We decided one afternoon to throw melon peels over the balcony. But not just throw them; we'd plan to do it as soon as we saw people exiting the building, so they'd get the load on their head. I peered over the balcony and aimed it directly at this woman's shoulder, and once I dropped it we quickly hid behind the bannister. I remember hearing loud protestations of disgust, which I took to mean my aim was perfect. We didn't think much of it until dad came home and gave us an earful. We were contrite, but I just couldn't understand how she knew which floor the peels were dropped from. But we were the only kids in the building, so it was an easy guess. I suspect my dad thought it was quite funny, even if he tried to act like the responsible parent.

Whenever he came to see us in São José, I particularly remember the time he had to leave. My mum would drive him to the bus station, and it was usually Sunday evening. It wasn't a cheerful time, for either of us. For me it was also because I would have to go to school the next day, which was a Monday, my least favourite day of the week. It was an unsettled feeling, like I knew I hadn't done homework properly, or I'd done it in a rush to get rid of it as soon as possible. The next day we'd be having breakfast at 6am and the school van would beep at around 630am. Off we'd go, on the yellow VW campervan with 5 more unhappy looking children. Our school had a strong Portuguese tradition, which in short meant it was pretty strict. One of the subjects was Moral and Civic Education, which I later learned had something to do with the military being in power. I found it incredibly dull, but in hindsight I can see the value of teaching kids how to behave in the world, provided they had a strong family unit to back it up.

I had an arts teacher in my first year of secondary school who I wouldn't call the most inspiring person to ever teach arts – she was probably very young, fresh out of college or university, having to deal with a group of around 20 mostly behaved kids, plus 10 tearaways sat at the back of the class, getting into trouble on a daily basis. Her name was Beatriz, she had a round face with long brown hair and light blue eyes, and always wore a round pendant necklace which had a sort of liquid spirit level on it. I was fascinated by her 'elf princess' vibe. We didn't do any actual art as far as I remember, it was more like lessons about art. Our classroom had a picture of the Brazilian president over the top of the blackboard. At that time, it was General Emilio Garrastazu Medici (likely another Italian second generation immigrant), who had a whiff of Ray Milland about him, with piercing blue eyes and his military accolades on his army coat. This was still, of course, in the middle of the military dictatorship. Beatriz would appeal to his authority when we were being particularly naughty in classroom, and that cold blue stare (the president's, not our teacher's) would actually make us go quiet.

I have fond but strange memories of that school. I'll probably cover some of them on my childhood chapter, which I mean to close at the end of my 12th year, sticking to the advent of teen age at year 13. Every day we had to hand out our personal notebook IDs to old Pereira, the school janitor who welcomed all kids via the narrow entrance gate. He used to rubber stamp 'present' next to whichever week day it was. If we missed school for one day, he'd rubber stamp 'absent' on the week day we missed. He looked mean, but he was actually quite a warm person, with a twinkle in his eye. Our school times were morning only, with a break in the middle. The patio area was split into various corners, some of which had demarcated hopscotch templates for break play, but you had to be quick to grab one of the 3 on the entire patio. We couldn't just grab a piece of chalk and draw our own: that was banned. There was also a small canteen which sold Fanta or Coca-Cola, cheese bread and small hot dogs. I rarely bought food on breaks, because we'd normally have some sort of packed snack, besides which we'd get a huge lunch on our return to my grandmother's house. I'd mostly sit on my own, watching the energetic effervescence of kids and teens running around the patio, most times in peace, but sometimes an altercation broke out, which required old Pereira to intervene.

Those weren't the happiest years of my life, and I believe this is the case for most people. My body took an eternity to mature, and I would experience a strange discomfort in seeing girls of a similar age develop breasts whilst I remained a dumpy child with, in a further humiliation, brown rimmed glasses. I think my mum wanted me to wear braces as well, but I refused this triple whammy of adolescent torture. I kept myself away from most girls from my class, especially the ones who looked like young ladies. I felt alien to them. I was essentially a loner, but would gravitate towards oddballs, dumpy girls like me, or anyone who didn't fit in for some reason. Occasionally I'd spend time with nice kids who were also very popular and got the highest grades. If I think back to them, it strikes me that it was a mystery; they seemed to get on with everyone and discriminate against no one. But other kids were not so nice. I remember this girl, Sandra, similar age to mine, who was vivacious and cheeky, and wore a spinal brace support. It's the sort of thing that would invite bullying or prejudice, but she was one of the popular pupils. She had an answer for everything and an on-off romance with another boy in our class. She lived their romance like a TV soap, on show for everyone to see. I admired in her everything I thought I lacked. But she could be cruel, as I found out one day. I stayed behind in class one day, during break, probably reading a book, which is what I did with any spare time I had. I hadn't noticed, but Sandra had stayed behind chatting in a low voice to her best friend Vania. They were sat on the other side, a few rows back from me. Suddenly she asked in a loud voice, "Luciana, do you have a boyfriend?". No one had ever asked me that before. I barely had time to think of what to say, because she answered her own question by saying "of course you don't, dumpy and ugly as you are!". Vania was as shocked as I was, and I heard her protesting, but this is another of those moments in life that I'd remember forever, as a snapshot. It was a mixed bag of feelings: here's a person I admired who turns out is horrible, but I admire her, so she must be right, and oh my I have felt dumpy and ugly recently so she's probably right, but I hate her for saying it. In fact, it was like a tumble dryer of conflicting emotions. Whatever it was, it crystallized a certain perception I had of myself, which took years to overcome. But it wasn't just due to peers' petty cruelty: my mother also wanted us to look like dancers, and we didn't, but felt the constant pressure to please her. And whilst I mention children's cruelty, I can't really complain much about Sandra's callousness given that I myself exercised a similar cruelty towards another class mate.

This must have been after the incident described above. There was a girl in our class who was a bit of an oddball, looking a bit tall and grown up for the year she was in. Her name was Gisele, and she might also have ranked as slightly 'dumpy' by Sandra's standards. She was blonde and geeky, but we got on well and I had been to her house for studies. She was the spitting image of her dad, a second-generation Polish immigrant, and they were very nice to me. I think she also found it hard to fit in, but mostly she had a sense of humour. One day, the assignment for our Grammar lesson was to write a poem or paragraph about the school, or family, or people close to us. I decided to write a slightly *picaresque* comic poem about the people in my class. I had some form in doing these sorts of assignments and the teacher knew I could do it pretty well. I wrote a scathing critique of the characters who stood out for me in class, for one reason or another. I wrote a couple of lines about Gisele on it. It was short, probably an eight-sentence short poem. I thought we'd just hand it in and that would be the end of it. But our teacher – called Socrates, a homonym of the ancient Athenian – had read my creations out loud to class before (he was amused by my 'style') and decided to do the same this time. I didn't think much of it. I had written the poem as a joke, thinking that nothing in it was contentious. But when I heard the lines about Gisele out loud my heart sank. I had written something very cruel about her physical appearance and the impact of what I wrote landed when I heard it. And when I turned to Gisele, a few seats to my right, she had her eyes lowered and her whole face was red and slumped down. If the impact of betrayal had a face, I was looking straight at it. Was I looking at myself when I heard Sandra's words? Was this how the world turned, an eye for an eye? Except it was someone else's eye. I felt deeply ashamed, even as the pupils applauded my witty words. But there were probably only me and Gisele in that classroom who knew the value of lost friendship, because that's what happened. Gisele later changed classes and left the school, I think. I never saw her again. But that unkind act lingered in my mind. The strangest thing was that, after I had left that school I somehow found Sandra's address and wrote to her, after my dad was transferred to Ecuador as Naval attaché. What did I write? Just pleasant platitudes, as if she and I had been friends and the dumpy insult had never happened. A sort of dysfunctional Stockholm syndrome-type pen friendship developed for a few letters, because she replied a few times, always very friendly and warm. Maybe she had felt guilty and was happy for the opportunity to make up for it. But I didn't mention it and neither did she. The correspondence eventually died down. But I never heard from Gisele again.

The dawn of teen age seemed to be a distant storm outlining itself on the horizon, a faint watercolour sketch of grey clouds, with a pallid sun hiding behind them. I didn't know what I was doing, going to school every day. I liked certain subjects and hated others. The whole business of learning seemed to be a navigation between knowledge which was welcome once understood, and the negotiation between nascent personalities. I still remember some of the more prominent kids, because of the way they presented themselves. But this in itself could be misleading, because a very assertive child does not translate into a very assertive adult. With my sister and cousins there was a permanent psychological tug of war. My cousin would team up with my sister and 'conspire' against me, which is to say they probably had a bit more in common and were definitely more street smart than me. I found it slightly offensive that my younger cousin could be more world weary than me. How did that happen? They were both a lot more interested in boys than I was. I was always a late developer, and really enjoyed playing with dolls until well after what I considered a normal age to be doing that sort of thing. I kept my dolls and played with them in hiding, like a dirty secret, fearful that I'd be found out and made fun of. But when I'd just engage in play, I found plenty of rhyme and reason to carry on, if only I could be left in peace to do it. On one of the rare occasions when the three of us were playing and running around my grandma's house, I stepped into my mother's bathroom and spotted a bag of panty liners. I didn't know what they were and asked my sister about it. I was genuinely surprised at the level of scorn I received from her and my cousin. Hang on a second, you're younger than me and you KNOW what this is for? They couldn't believe how naïve I was. My mother was in the next room and heard the kerfuffle. She told them both off (not the best strategy for my future credibility) and they left. She then gently explained what a panty liner was for. But it was a bit too gentle and I was even more confused. Women bleed? How, why? You mean I will bleed at some point? Does it hurt? She didn't have much time and said I'd learn more as the time came. And come it did, although it was quite late, by any standards. I was 15, on a student exchange in London, and at the National Gallery looking at old masters' paintings. But that's for the next chapter.

It's curious how I don't really remember a lot of my birthday parties from my childhood. I remember both parties from my 2 years in the north of Brazil, I guess because we had so much fun despite having to go to a school we hated. Well, we hated it at first as their teaching method was so different from the cushy American tap-dancing nuns. But we learned to appreciate it and even find it humorous, probably because we knew we wouldn't be there for long. Our parents took us on a few trips around the state of Bahia and even beyond. We were taken to Ilhéus and Itabuna, a couple of small towns near the coast, made famous by Jorge Amado's novel *Gabriela, Clove & Cinnamon.* It was the main national hub for cocoa bean production, and we were invited to visit a farm belonging to one of the largest local growers. I don't remember so much about the trip, except for the exhilaration of our car entering the massive plantation, the main dust road cutting through the trees like a terracotta artery, me and my sister sat in the back of our white *Variant* winding our windows down to feel the hot evening air and see the sun setting behind row upon row of cocoa bean trees, and the smell…an overpowering scent of cocoa entered our nostrils and our sentient beings like nothing before. It was chocolate, but it was more chocolate than real chocolate. It comforted, seduced and slapped our senses all at the same time. Later, as we arrived and got settled in our rooms, it wasn't like any farm I had seen before. All interiors and walls were wood panelled but modern looking, like a business hotel. Now that I write this it suddenly strikes me that our navy house at the base was also mostly wood panelled.

Summers in Bahia were very hot and dry with a bit of a breeze if near the sea. Throughout our 2 years there I only remember the warm weather and very little rain. Lots of sun, always. Even during autumn and winter, which in Brazil fall around April & May. During Easter egg hunts we were prompted to find our haul soon, because there was no telling how long the chocolate treats would last before melting into their cellophane wrapping and down the tree trunks. They were usually hanging rather low from tall trees which circled the entire house, wrapped in colourful papers. I once found a message signed by the chief Easter bunny herself (it was gendered) with best wishes and requests that we be good girls this coming year. But the chief Easter bunny's handwriting looked suspiciously like my mum's, which helped break the spell around Christmas and other children's longed-for celebrations. For me, at least. My sister wasn't so forensically minded and didn't notice the similarity. I didn't want to shatter her illusion. At least not until she was mean to me again.

Bahia was the first coastal state sighted by the Portuguese explorers in the 1500s, and as such there was a lot of history to it, mostly of a violent nature. We were too young to understand it, even if it was part of the school curriculum. But the fact that Bahia's population was probably around 65% or more black and mixed race told its own tale. The state had been one of the main hubs for the docking of slave ships with its dreadful cargo, which would then be sold and distributed around the country. Where we were, the main slave labour had been on sugar cane plantations. More to the south, mining and coffee. I don't remember any sugar cane or tobacco plantations around where we lived, because most of the big farms had been further north, in Pernambuco. Growing up in the south, the only black people in our immediate circle were our nanny Eunice and one of my grandmother's kitchen maids. And they were both from Bahia. At my secondary school I only remember this one mixed race kid, Kaká, quite small for his size, who we used to hang out with. One of the other kids teased him by using a racial slur. Kaká didn't seem to take offence and responded with quite a funny and witty takedown. The incident resolved itself, but I can't help thinking Kaká must have heard similar insults many times, whereas the other kid probably hadn't.

At our school in Bahia there were two black girls, sisters, always immaculate. I am trying to remember their names, but only Vilma or Velma come to mind. They both wore delicate tiny silver earrings and I suspect they were from a well-to-do family. They were fairly quiet kids, and all their exuberance came out at the school gates, after class: they would be the first to get treats from the white-lace-clad *baiana* sellers outside, eating their spicy prawn *acarajés* on the way home. Back at the Navy base, we had maids and a gardener who were black. But my father also had a colleague, a fellow Navy officer, who was black. Most kids around our age at the base were officer's children, and we more or less gathered together, without much thought to affinity or preference. One of the black officer's daughters played with us often. Her name was Georgia. But there was also another Georgia, so to avoid confusion we referred to them as Little White Georgia and Little Black Georgia. It was innocent enough and they didn't seem to mind, but who knows what lies in the hearts of people? Little

Black Georgia's dad was also a great jazz pianist and a good guy, according to my father. When I heard he'd been posted to the USA and our family back to SP I had a bit of a racist reaction. I asked my mother "how come black people get the raffle ticket before us??" Much like the story about the homeless when I was five, this episode was repeated to family more or less flagging my snobbery at such a young age. I don't actually remember saying that, but I do remember thinking it. I now remember that our nanny used to call me Sour Whitey because I had really white skin, cried at the drop of a hat (especially when I was defeated at board games) and was a bit "fussy". She called my sister "Blacky" because she seemed to have gotten the middle eastern/ Northern gene pool. I didn't like being called Sour Whitey because to me it sounded and looked like curdled milk. I had a much higher opinion of myself but I was a snob and an elitist – even my sister would accuse me of that…To talk about this now, in writing, is a bit shame inducing but I have come to believe that I will not banish my Shadow as if it was a leper because in doing that I miss the chance of understanding and integrating it.

When she was a teenager, my mother had completed a cake baking and decorating course, and I vividly remember the birthday cakes she used to bake us, up until we were teens ourselves. While we still lived in the north of Brazil, for my 8th birthday she not only baked my birthday cake but also decorated the main table herself. She baked a *Nega Maluca* cake, which roughly translates as 'crazy negress'. In the polarized days we live in I realise this might be analogous to the N word and therefore racist, but as times change and words become contentious, I think it is important not to ban language, provided it is inserted in the appropriate context. This recipe had been thus named around the 1840s, and there are two versions of this story: In the first, a slave woman accidentally dropped a whole bag of cocoa powder into a plain cake recipe. She tried to excuse herself, but no one could understand what she said (she was African) - but they liked the cake. In the second version, the slave was mixing the ingredients and instead of milk and butter she used hot water and oil. Which, for an 1840s housewife, was obviously crazy. But going back to the cake, back in the 70s, surrounded by school friends and high on Fanta, I absolutely loved my mother's culinary results. We had a round mahogany table which she decked with red cellophane paper, with red bows all around the rims.

She also made trays of *brigadeiros,* a highly popular Brazilian sweet made with condensed milk, cocoa powder and hundreds and thousands. The centre piece was the cake: a two-tier chocolate sponge (I don't even know if it was the *Nega Maluca!*) decorated as a black woman's face, with added gold hoop earrings, raisins for hair and strawberry cream in the shape of a mouth. I think there's even a picture of the whole birthday set up before the kids demolished it. I don' think anyone in their right mind would reproduce this decoration now but try as I might I cannot find a reason why this could be offensive. My mother never baked a cake with a white or Asian woman's face. But that's probably because there is no such recipe in the annals of Brazilian cooking. For a country which consists almost entirely of a mixed-race population, Brazil has a strange relationship with racism. I said previously that we hardly ever hung out with black kids, except for our nanny's sons - and they were much younger than us, in any case. We were lower middle class and went to private schools, but that's because they weren't that expensive and state schools were considered very poor quality. Anyone with a few bob could and would send their kids to a private school. Seeing a dark-skinned child in those schools was rare. My cousin Amélia once rebelled and decided her dad shouldn't spend that much money on their education (she is one of four) and so decided, of her own accord, to enrol at a local state school. This was probably her early secondary education. She didn't stay long, maybe a year, because her dad made her go back to private school. But during the time she was at a state school I remember her hanging out with a lot of more mixed-race kids. I never witnessed racism within my family, but not being around a lot of black people except for servants meant that it was the expected social contract. Writing about this is a bit uncomfortable, like walking through a minefield, as if I could at some point say something inappropriate. But I'm willing to take the risk, if I am to be honest with myself.

And now that I am in the middle of this minefield, I will also mention one of my dad's friends at the time in Bahia, a large man called Antonio. He always invited us to gargantuan barbecue parties, and he was usually the one who ate the most. Dad's friendship with Antonio was a little bit conflicting, because he thought the guy talked too much, ate too much and drank too much. He would also visit us sometimes, always bringing a massive slab of rump steak for a quick barbecue. Whenever he visited he would bring his son, a kid called Érico, who looked and acted nothing like his dad. He was thin, a bit older than us and even in the heat of Bahia he would wear short sleeved shirts with a crochet waist coat that looked more like a multi-coloured vest. This look was rounded off by bell bottom polyester trousers and slightly higher heels than would be normal for a kid. His hair was like a Chanel bob. Érico must have been around 12, so around 3 years older than most of us. When he played with us he would always think up these elaborate schemes, whereby he would be the owner of a small circus and he would fantasize about what attractions he would have. Sometimes he'd act out what was on his mind. For the rest of us this would be a very odd choice of play. What was wrong with chasing each other around the beach or hide and seek? One of the older boys then started to spread the 'rumour' that Érico was gay. Which probably wasn't the word used then and I'm sure that's not what was said; it was probably something a bit similar to 'effeminate'. I didn't know what that meant, but from the context presented to us it was meant to be something embarrassing. I could tell Érico wasn't like the other boys, but I liked him because he made us laugh. I understood the meaning of outrageous before I knew the word, because of how Érico acted. But after this half-baked outing, suddenly it wasn't OK to be around him anymore, like he had something contagious. It was never spelled out and no one was mean to him, but all of a sudden Érico and his dad stopped coming to the house. I heard my parents mentioning Antonio and his son, as if wondering how such a macho Brazilian could have such a "delicate flower" for a son. My dad said he felt a bit sorry for Antonio and how disappointing it must have been to have a son like that. And this was my introduction to different sexualities. My family were essentially good compassionate generous people, but this attitude to homosexuality was clearly ingrained in their generation.

But my dad also had a second cousin called Edelton, from the family branch which actually hailed from Bahia. I've never met him, and he's passed away a long time ago, but he was sort of 'famous' for being an outrageously camp Carnival star (or 'carnivalesque' as it was known back then). He would always appear on the cover of Manchete, the biggest weekly magazine at the time, during carnival season, along with a couple of other big names in the field. There were always extravagant contests for carnival costumes, and Edelton would always win first prize on the

Deluxe category. He designed and made his own costumes, which probably took him a whole year in between Carnival Balls. They were immaculate, fabulous and mad, like a Swarovski dream on speed. He'd be covered head to toe in feathers and bling, in a highly elaborate costume which indeed looked like it took months to craft. I don't think anyone in the family knew for sure if he was gay, but that was the assumption, given his occupation. But my dad was rather proud of this cousin, because, in his words, he was quite discreet and didn't flaunt it!

The other family member who was talked about in that respect was my mum's cousin Fabio, who had lived in their house with his other siblings since their parents died of cancer. It was funny how they talked about him in later years, like 'it was complicated'. Fabio had actually had an unusual life after leaving my grandmother's house. He was much older than us and he was gone way before we moved in. He went to Europe and lived in Amsterdam for a few years, designing rings, jewellery and leather bags. Later I heard he'd got ill and had to be brought back to Brazil. My grandmother sent him a ticket and so he moved back in for a while. I remember when he'd just arrived, quite stylish in cowboy boots, black jeans and a silver satin dinner jacket with small black stars. And long hair and moustache, like a member of the Grateful Dead. He smelled of leather and sandalwood, which from that point on I always associated with Holland, up until my first stays in Amsterdam confirmed that it was just a childhood memory. One of my mother's uncles was also a man I always associated with the smell of leather and men's cologne. His name was Riccardo and he was married to mum's aunt Rania (nod to the Syrian clan here). He was handsome, incredibly well dressed at all times, and was always smoking, leaving a trail of Paco Rabanne and Marlboros. I have this image of Riccardo as a 70s advert for men's clothes; he had longish brown hair, wore impeccable khaki ensembles and brown leather boots. I always thought he was a total mismatch to his wife, who looked to me a bit frumpy and old enough to be his mum. Riccardo died relatively young, not yet 60, of throat cancer. Illness had been almost a constant in our family, with quite a few people dying of cancer and a couple others being alcoholics, which hastened their demise.

The Italians were highly emotional and outspoken, even if my great grandfather didn't quite conform to this stereotype – he was cautious and single minded in his approach to life and business. On my grandmother Helena's side, the Swiss and the Syrian had contributed to a high degree of drama. Our Swiss ancestors came to Brazil under difficult circumstances, around half of the people on those ships perished during the journey, leaving a lot of despondent and grieving people arriving at a completely new environment. Some died later, of tropical fevers or childbirth. Those that remained married amongst themselves, as they seemed already united in grief. A generational wave of depression must have passed on to my grandmother's family. I know she and her 8 brothers and sisters were disciplined with beatings, as was probably the preferred method back in the early 1900s. But she always said her Syrian/American father never beat them, only their Swiss mother. In fact, she told me a funny story once: that her father Wadia would tell his wife he was going to punish the children, then he'd take them into a room, take out his belt and hit the furniture, whilst telling the kids to do a bit of pretend crying. Apparently, this worked for a while, until his wife became suspicious of one of the kids' scandalous overacting and decided to resume punishing them herself. I met this great grandmother. She was very old and lived at her daughter's until she died. She was still very strict and frankly a bit scary. When I went to Switzerland, I saw many old ladies who looked exactly like her, hair up on a bun and always a brooch over a jumper.

But my great grandfather Wadia was a soft man who'd had quite a full life: aged 14, back in Beirut, he rebelled against his widowed father, a high-ranking government official, because of his marriage to a new bride. He was at boarding school but ran away and joined a circus. They toured all over Europe, with his dad's private agents trailing the kid to make sure he was OK. At some point his father let him be, thinking that he was old enough to make his own destiny. That was probably the ethos with regards to runaway children back in late 19th century. At the age of seventeen, Wadia boarded a US bound ship and probably arrived at Ellis Island. Somehow, he made his way up to Rhode Island, where he enlisted on Company H of the 1st Rhode Island Volunteer Infantry, which became active in combat duties during the Spanish-American war of 1898. He was wounded a few times, and my grandmother told me of some horrible stories of enemies he faced in body combat. He probably had PTSD for the rest of his life, but at the time it wasn't diagnosed so he had to endure almost daily nightmares and a weak heart. When the war ended he moved down to Georgia, where he got himself a plot of land, a new business and an American fiancée. But then he got the travel bug again, and I don't know how it happened, but he ended up in Rio de Janeiro. There he met Dorothea, the Swiss immigrant he'd marry one month later, leaving his American life behind for good.

I would have loved to meet him, and also my Italian entrepreneur great grandad Benedetto. My grandmother always told me stories about her upbringing, her childhood, her time at boarding school (which she had to leave in order to help out at home), and her early married life. I loved hearing her stories, and not only what she said but also how she said it. She had a way of weaving a yarn through words, and the words conjured up images, and she breathed life into the characters, making different voices, and the cadence and pitch of her voice kept me entranced for hours. I would always ask for more, and sometimes she would tell me the same stories, but I loved hearing them again and again. It awakened the passion for storytelling in me, and how hypnotic it could be.

I haven't mentioned my father's family so much, perhaps because we didn't spend so much time around them. I did mention that I wasn't particularly keen on my paternal grandmother, because of her favouritism. I 'sort of' liked visiting her and my grandfather Raposo, mostly because their home was a mystery to me, and I liked mysteries. I wasn't sure why anyone would choose to have the entire kitchen furniture in red Formica, plus cooker and fridge also red. She wasn't even a socialist. They had one of those old black Bakelite wall mounted telephones which made a tingling sound when dialled. I wondered why it had a brown rope as a cord, instead of plastic like other phones. Despite being right next to a bright sitting room, her dining room was dark and full of deep green marble objects. There was a small garden at the front, next to which my grandfather's car, an old DKV, was usually parked. Upstairs, I liked to nose around their bedroom, which had an old furniture set I was told they got as a wedding present sometime in the 1920s. There were two single beds, an added puzzle to me given that my maternal grandparents had a king size bed. Next to their bedroom was my grandfather Raposo's office, which I only entered a couple of times in his lifetime. He sometimes sat there, at his desk, surrounded by bookshelves on every wall. The walls were green, the books mostly mud coloured and he seemed to have acquired a brownish green hue to his skin as well. He was small and quiet, and I never got to know him properly. As for my grandmother Edith, I didn't really get to know her either. They both passed away when I was on my late teens and not terribly interested in people who (I assumed) weren't interested in me either.

I have asked my father about them, and his memories are more vivid about his mum. He told me he enlisted in Naval College at 18 in order to get away from her. He had to go to Rio to study and moved in with an aunt. His mum was a domineering character and even at an old age I could tell she had a strong personality, which is one of the reasons she didn't get on with my grandma Helena, who was certainly a force of nature. During a house decluttering exercise at my mum's recently I found an old letter she wrote me and my sister, when she was visiting her eldest granddaughter at college in Strasbourg, France. I was surprised at the wicked sense of humour coming through on the short sentences, but even more surprised at sensing a totally different personality from what I remembered. I had viewed her my entire life through the lens of my opinion as a child, and what others said about her, but now it was too late to find out what she was really like.

I meant to complete the childhood part of this book round about now. I don't know if I will succeed because more memories are bound to crop up as I move on to my teenage years and how immigration and film have formed such an essential part of who I have become. I realise my entire family have come from other countries. Perhaps with the possible exception of my grandmother Edith, whose father was Portuguese, but whose mother was a *cabocla*, which could mean someone from mixed race Native indigenous origin or even African. Whichever it is, I come from a long bloodline of people who moved around to pursue a life they dreamed of, or to escape a life they had nightmares about or that no longer served them. I didn't think twice when the opportunity came to spend a few months in London. I felt stifled where I was, my career wasn't going anywhere, and my love life was inexistent. As a matter of fact, the impulse was to follow a Scottish guy I had met on the personal columns – this was before the internet, of course. I didn't have a plan. I didn't set for the airport thinking I'd settle in the UK and marry and remain here for the next 23 years. If I had glimpsed the future I might have been a bit spooked. But during my childhood I can only think of coming across the tap-dancing nuns or the McAllister family, or Patty's US Barbies as markers – and triggers - of my fascination with foreign lands and cultures.

ON TEEN AGE

I didn't feel that much different once I entered my teenage years. There was even a slight reluctance to grow up, because the world of older kids seemed scary to me. I got on better with adults than with teenagers my own age. I somehow felt I hadn't made the most of my time as a child and so I wished to extend it. And I watched as most girls around me excitedly shared the growth of breasts or the thrill of their first boyfriend. I can't even remember when I got my first bra, but it was likely around 14 years of age because I don't recall having any hint of a breast before then. My first bras were actually hand made by my grandmother Helena, who crochet-wove them! But to be frank they were more wishful thinking appendages than the real thing, because there was nothing to encase by that point. It was more a psychological tool to get us used to wearing the real thing. I was very conscious of breast sizes at school, they seemed to vary a lot within one classroom full of 13 and 14-year- old girls. Boys probably had that feeling as well, they either looked muscly and tall whereas the year before they didn't, or they were like me, feeling like nothing had changed and still having the attitude and appearance of a child.

The trickiest thing for me to navigate was the nascent desire between sexes, or at least the awareness that there was a thrill whenever a certain person walked by. I only remember this boy, Paulo, who I had a crush on during early secondary school. He wasn't at the same class as me, but I'd spotted him during break. He was small and looked more like a child than a young man, but I guess that was my preference back then. I never spoke to him and wouldn't have dreamed of even trying. I would watch him during breaks, and at the end watched him go back inside. Only once I went over to his classroom after break just to get a glimpse of him in his 'habitat', but no one noticed me – I would have been mortified if they had! I also had a girl crush on a younger girl called Alma. She was on the year below me, and I found out her full name after some research, much like I'd done with Paulo. I was developing a sort of stalker-lite talent so to speak. But my crushes were mostly platonic, and if either of them had spoken to me I would have frozen, like what happened a couple of years later when we moved to Ecuador. But that's for another chapter.

We were still living at my grandmother's house, but things were getting a bit fraught as my sister fully embraced adolescence and all its foibles. Outside school, I was usually stuck at home reading or day dreaming. I don't know how my sister managed to meet so many different people. We were enrolled in dance academy for a term, with a bit of classical ballet and jazz lessons keeping us busy. The dance teacher was an old Russian woman called Madam Kostova. Much later I found out she'd been a protégé of the Nijinskis, but back then I had nothing but fear and contempt for her. She stood, in leotard, low heels and a stick, with her grey hair up, marking up the tempo and giving us a right telling off when she noticed some deterioration of balletic posture. I would get that stick on my bum a few times because I'd forgotten to suck my tummy in, or I wasn't paying enough attention. It was clear I was never going to be a classical ballerina, but I did like dancing. I still do, but on the threshold of my teen life it wasn't much fun being constantly made an example of. The academy had an open day for parents to come watch the results of our efforts, and luckily my mum came in on a day when we had jazz lessons, which I really liked. She was open mouthed, and later told me she had no idea I could dance so well. I thought she was trying to encourage me, but I'd already decided Madam Kostova's method was too unforgiving for me, so she agreed to let me quit. Sometimes I wish I'd stayed on, but the vision of a child is never so far into the future. The thought of dancing lingers on in my mind, and when I do dance I feel a strange sort of liberation.

Sometimes we'd spend a day or two at my grandma Edith's house, where my sister kept a real gang of people at her beck and call. These were all neighbourhood kids, who would start ringing the bell as soon as we arrived, drawn in by seemingly mysterious sources, because these were the days before mobiles or internet. Feeling a little out of my element, I thought I'd rather hang out with my sister and her friends than sit around my half deaf grandfather or domineering grandmother. But the tragedy of it was that my sister didn't want me to hang around. She called me her 'tail'. One of her friends, a boy called Hamilton, was a bit more inclined to welcome me into the fold, but he was a minority: she had turned them all against my being there! Or at least that's what I thought. There wasn't much to do anyway, just hang around outside one of the kids' family home, or go over to the bakery for ice cream, or, even better, have a milk shake at the nearest hamburger place. And smoke a few fags, which I could never successfully do. I felt a bit like a blank slate, and because I wanted to belong, I thought I needed to copy their preferences, or at least emulate them occasionally.

I had seen my sister joining the 'rebels' in the back of the room (in Portuguese it was called '*fundão*'), whereas the CDFs would always sit at the front. CDF was an acronym for *cú de ferro,* which translates as 'iron asshole'. It meant kids who always got good grades and actually paid attention during class. I always picked a seat next to the wall, between third and fourth row. I knew I'd never be a CDF because I wasn't that committed to getting top grades, but also because there was something slightly odd about it, like if you were a CDF you were the simultaneous object of envy and scorn. But I lacked the guts to be a full-time member of the backroom posse. It wasn't just that I lacked guts, but those kids were viewed as glamorous losers and I wasn't willing to nail such colours to my mast just yet. Not that I knew it consciously, but something stopped me, even though they seemed to be having a lot of fun. So, a secondary school classroom becomes a microcosm of society in my memory, but that's how it was.

My sister was also part of the after-school smoking club, which was basically a gang of kids having a cigarette outside, after school hours. We had to hang around waiting for all stragglers to come out, so we could board Cleberson's tatty yellow VW anyway, so plenty of time for light mischief. There was a candy man outside, and I'd use up any change left from my break snack purchase to buy some lollies. My sister would join the smoking club, who were basically kids who looked like they had a collective chip on their shoulder, attempting to look really cool whilst trying to balance it. I'm sure it was all posing, because when my sister took pity on me and let me have a drag I actually inhaled, and the nicotine nearly made me faint. I hated the taste. The old janitor Pereira looked at us disapprovingly. I quite liked him and I'm sure he cared about those kids, not wanting to see them develop what he would consider a bad habit. There were a couple of quirky characters in that school, which for starters was called Luís de Camões, after its namesake, the legendary Iberian poet, Portugal's answer to *Don Quixote*'s Cervantes. Mr DeLucca was the headmaster, inspecting the school grounds with a critical eye, even during breaks. My sister didn't like him, because he had a habit of gently disciplining her to make it look like he wanted the best for her. Which was probably true, but he wasn't very good at disguising his patronising tone. On top of which, he always wore a three-piece silk suit, whatever the occasion and weather. He moved in a slightly odd manner, with the front ends of his suit flapping about and his short arms suspended in the air, like a clueless slow-motion T-Rex.

I generally sought to stay out of trouble, but my sister had no such concerns. She once set someone's arse on fire because he made fun of her hairy legs. Well, she nearly did – he was sat in front of her and she had a lighter under his bottom until he jumped off his seat screaming. She was called to DeLucca's office to be disciplined, which meant calling in parents to disclose offense details. But this time even my father could not hide the amusement in his face when told of her latest exploit. She was never a big trouble maker – at least not at school. I talk about my sister a lot in these pages. That's because she's always been a big influence in my life, someone I simultaneously admired and scorned. I'd find myself wondering sometimes, how did she get away with doing some of the things she came up with? I'd be split between envying her fearlessness or lamenting her foolishness. In my early teens I guess I lived through her, by proxy. I observed the world, fearful of putting a foot wrong, and most times decided it was safer to stay in my book bubble. Was it because of the time I spoke out so frankly as a toddler and got labelled a little monster? Maybe, but whatever the reason, I must have thought self-expression was a dangerous business. It has echoed through my life but given me other skills as well. I've never asked my sister what she thought of me back then, but if she reads this book I'm bound to get my answer.

Around that time, and on Mother's Day, she decided to run away to join a hippie commune. We didn't know that's where she'd gone because she just disappeared. I don't remember exactly why, but I think it was because there was talk of my dad taking a post as Navy attaché in Ecuador for a couple of years, and this was likely her way of rebelling. I don't actually have a strong memory of how this unfolded, but her trail had not gone warm before my dad realised there was only one place she could have tried to seek shelter at: his mother's beach house. Him and mum drove down to the coast to meet the caretaker, who told them my sister had dropped by but gone on to Ilha Grande, the big island opposite the village. She can't have been older than 15 or 16, so their worry was probably justified. Ilha Grande is actually not that big and it would have been easy to ask around the small fishing villages dotted around its perimeter. They eventually found her at a big house, which was rented out to a group of people (hippies, according to my dad) who were artists and crafts people. She was a bit surprised to see them, but declared she was happy there and wanted to live a free life among kindred spirits. They could have legally dragged her back home, but my mum figured she'd only run off again, so they left her there. I was told my dad cried on the drive back, clearly not quite equipped to deal with stroppy teens. He was always a deeply emotional person. My mother, of a more practical nature, deduced that my sister would eventually return home once she needed money or care. Which is what eventually happened. She had bad toothache, and nowhere to go for it, not locally. There were dentists on the main land, but she had no money, so she did come back. Not with her tail between her legs, in fact it was pretty much business as usual.

It would have been around this time that my uncle Saulo's wife suggested that my mum referred me and my sister to her diet doctor. We noticed that she'd slimmed down a great deal, but at least I wasn't aware that there was any great need for us to lose weight. Not to that level anyway. It was a pretty strict diet, with one of the daily meals being a vegetable soup that had no taste whatsoever. This was hard for a family of food lovers. I remember my first consultation with Dr Teodoro, the slimming wizard. I don't remember much about this first time, except that he said he could tell I was one of those people who sat in front of the TV eating chocolate and getting fat. Although I don't remember the reaction, my mum later told me she saw big fat tears rolling down my face. Even my tears were fat! She probably thought she was doing us a favour, stopping us from being overweight forever. That was likely Dr Teodoro's intention as well, tough love. But what happened is that me and my sister started a life-long cycle of constant dieting and acute awareness of our body shape. My mother had always been thin, despite 2 pregnancies, and I know she longed for us to have 'dancer bodies'. Her acute focus on body shape has passed on to us, but don't we all absorb some ontological filter from those closest to us? If I think back to when she took me to see this doctor, I had a sudden jump in weight at around 14. I think I had a subconscious refusal to grow up, like Peter Pan, and being overweight might make me look less like a teenage girl. I definitely had very strange leanings at the time. My preferences were reading (anything from Edgar Alan Poe or gothic novels) and watching reruns of The Monkees on TV. I had a total crush on Davy Jones, but at the same time I knew he probably looked much older now than on this 1960s series. No wonder my sister's friends ran a mile from me. These were the days when Saturday Night Fever came out, and all the young girls were gaga about John Travolta and the soundtrack. There were school dances or birthday parties which were awash with Bee Gees songs, disco soundtracks or even the tacky Brazilian versions of the big hits. My sister adopted a sort of classic disco hairdo, with a blow-dry-outwards like Tony Manero's doomed girlfriend Annette. But all her friends were also copying that hairdo – except me of course, because I hated the film, the music, everything. My opinion of it changed considerably once I got into filmmaking.

At this point we were living at our own home, a two-storey apartment in the heart of Pinhos, a mix of affluence and lower middle-class bonhomie, but my mum loved it because everything was available just around the corner. We'd left my grandmother's once the conflict between older and younger generation got too much for my parents. They knew we wouldn't stay there long, because my father had been posted to Ecuador, but my mum especially welcomed the feeling of having her own space. I didn't like it so much at first because nothing could be as spacious as my grandmother's house. But this was a big apartment, with 2 big living rooms, kitchen, laundry area and maid's room (ever present) on the ground floor, and 3 bedrooms and 2 bathrooms upstairs. It was also much closer to our school, so we didn't have to wake up so early. But the first few breakfasts without my grandmother's stern but loving hand were a bit of a shock to me. I could tell my mum was relieved, though. And I got used to it and actually grew to really like the new home. I had managed to infect my sister and her girlfriends with my Monkees crush, and so we all spent afternoons eating pancakes and watching reruns on TV. I had started writing and publishing my own newspaper, called *O Desbocado* (roughly translates as The Loose-Tongued). I had inherited my grandfather's typewriter, so I basically typed a few copies to be distributed to close family and friends. My paper usually had four A5 pages, with totally fabricated family news, jokes, poems, lonely hearts section, and police news. The butt of most of my jokes and articles was my sister, but to my surprise she didn't mind it because they always made her laugh. Sometimes she would instigate more news and articles to see how far I'd take it. We were getting a bit closer by this stage, and she didn't mind my hanging out with her friends that much anymore. But certain things she just would not share with me. She'd started going out with a boy named Ricky, a wannabe surfer a bit older than her. Surfing and skateboards were all the rage at the time, and no sane teenager would bypass some sort of affiliation to either. But I was not a sane teenager. I would make endless fun of Ricky, who had a dyed blonde bob half covering his eyes and was probably too skinny to keep his balance on a surf board. But he wasn't as dim as I thought. One day they both disappeared into my sister's room and no amount of knocking would elicit any response. The young girl who helped in the kitchen was starting to panic. I had no idea what was going on and even began to think they'd left without us noticing, but the door was locked. They were in there, and eventually walked out, my sister looking like nothing had happened. She never confirmed it, but years later I realised she'd popped her cherry on that day. But the spell seemed to have been broken because Ricky was out of the picture faster than you could say rip curl. At the time I had no clue what it all meant, and if anyone tried to explain it to me I would have been even more confused. I mean the mechanics of it, beyond the actual concept. These affairs were for older people, I told myself, and I just wasn't interested.

Around this time, we also happened to be sharing a friend, a new girl at school called Maria José. At first, we thought hers was a funny name – it translates as Mary Joseph, which obviously invited 'what happened to Jesus?'-type jokes. Later we realised she was from Portugal, where people have slightly unusual and old-fashioned names. She was an only daughter, quite sheltered, but didn't get along with her strict parents. Who were surprisingly small, like Hobbits, as we found out when we had at play day at their flat. She was deferent towards them, but not close. She also reverted to speaking with a Portuguese accent when they were around, which I found odd. I compared it to my own family dynamics and was surprised to see how free we were, despite all restrictions. But I liked Majo, as we called her. I liked her because she made no difference between me and my sister and treated us the same. She actually brought us closer in a very natural way. She totally got my sense of humour and my awkwardness and embraced them. We hung out a lot throughout our last year at secondary school and stayed in touch even after we'd left for Ecuador, in 1979. Before the internet or mobile phones there were letters, and I was always elated at the sight of them arriving on the doormat. There was an anticipation and craftsmanship about writing letters which millennials will never know. They would probably say there's similar sensations available with technology today, but it's not quite the same. There was a trinket shop which only Navy people had access to, where we used to buy imported letter writing paper and envelopes, usually US made. Most of the ones we bought had well known branded characters like Snoopy or Hello Kitty. It was a special ritual, picking specific brands for special people. Majo wrote to us faithfully, to me mostly as my sister wasn't so keen on writing. Teenage constancy is not particularly strong, and so our letters trickled down and finally stopped. But I had a whole new world in a new country. After a few months I did not miss her letters so much. I still keep most of my correspondence from that time and going through each letter again takes me back in time, like writing this book does. Years later, after we'd returned to São José and newer friends, I wondered what had become of Majo. My mother had heard some story about a Portuguese family of three having had an accident in which nobody survived, but I thought this was a bit unbelievable. No one I knew had ever had a similar fate, but I never heard from her again. The only other experience with death or injury I'd had, apart from my own finger, was a kid at primary school who I actually witnessed get injured on a see-saw during break. The impulse being greater than his own weight, he flew thru de air and got his head wedged over the opposing end of it, made of hollow metal bars. It sounds more horrific than it probably was, but I do have that image in my mind. Of looking down at the concrete slabs in the courtyard while kids ran around me amidst the cacophony of play and ambulance sirens and spotting a drop of blood on the ground. In that moment I felt the vulnerability of life, even if I could not yet add words to feeling.

And so, after a year in Pinhos we finally set off for Ecuador, but not before a bit of family drama over Christmas: after my grandmother Helena's traditional eve supper, my uncle Saulo decided to go for a spin on somebody's motorcycle, and my aunt went with him. It was already dark, and they'd both had a bit to drink. After a few glasses of Port and more chat, and running around for us kids, the delay in their return and the lack of any word started to get people rattled. There was no way to contact them. More time passed and by this stage Saulo's pregnant wife was completely stressed. Either my dad or my uncle Wilson, or both, drove one of the cars around the block to see if they could meet them. They were found on the road, passed out, after having had an accident when the bike skidded on loose asphalt. In the end an ambulance was called, and they both spent the night in hospital, Saulo's wife crying hysterically, to such a degree on hearing the news that my grandmother thought she might have the baby there and then. Nothing too serious happened to them in the end, although my uncle had some loose grains of asphalt lodged under the skin just below his eye, which took some plastic surgery to remedy. The one significant unspoken consequence of this event was that my uncle and my aunt became distant, never really regaining the rapport they'd previously had. No one ever mentioned anything, and it is a wild guess, but to me it seemed too much of a coincidence.

Uncle Saulo had an eventful childhood. My grandmother Helena got pregnant with him in the wake of her young daughter's death, and he was born into an environment of grief and despair. In a way, his birth helped alleviate this. But he started having psychic visions at the age of 2 or 3, usually crisis which lasted a few days and left him bedridden. He would speak of a man standing in the corner, who looked like Jesus but who had 'bad' eyes. Each time, and a few days after these visions started, the family priest would arrive to look after him, uncalled for. He just knew to come. This lasted for a few years, until my uncle reached 7 or 8 years old. The visions were gone, but he was changed. He was a very bright child. Probably what is known as an indigo child. He never wanted to speak of it again though; it was traumatic enough at the time. I've heard that psychic gifts must be developed but he ran from it all his life, which wasn't so happy in the end. He passed away as I am finishing this book. He was a mystery I might never decipher.

Our trip to Ecuador was eventful. My dad had travelled ahead of us, to find a home and settle into his new post. It had been really hard for him because his dad, my grandfather Raposo, was dying of prostate cancer. He delayed the journey for as long as he could, but eventually he had to leave. He went to see his father, and he knew he would not see him alive again. He spoke to the Navy chaplain, who comforted him as best he could, but essentially said 'you have a life to live'. My dad didn't share this with us so much, or perhaps he did but we were lost in the excitement of a new place.

We were given diplomatic passports and first-class tickets, which I thought was the height of sophistication. I remember champagne on the flight, but it can't have been us drinking as I was not 15 yet, unless my mum let us have a taste of it. When we landed, dad had been there for about a month, and arranged school places for us and temporary accommodation at a Navy facility. We were picked up by a Navy van and my dad was delighted to see us. I don't know what dark night of the soul he went through after his father's passing but seeing us again brought a smile to his face. The trip from the airport to the Naval Club was a bit under an hour, but we had a sort of culture shock. I'd been pretty excited to live abroad for a while, and I imagined this place to be somewhat similar to the US, which was my whole experience of what 'abroad' meant. This place looked nothing like what I'd been led to expect. It looked not dissimilar to the North of Brazil in terms of poverty and destitution, but it had a different flavour. And it smelled different as well, but not in a good way.

The Naval Club was a welcome distraction from the ugly visual sores of Guayaquil, the coastal city which would be our home for the next 2 years. Dad hadn't managed to find a good home for us yet, so we settled into this place, which was a sports club frequented mostly by Navy officers and some well-to-do Ecuadorians. It had two residents' blocks, a bit like a hotel, but most of it was sports facilities. The best thing about it was the swimming pool, which was huge, with shallow areas for kids and a deep section with diving boards. It was surrounded by what was called the 'social' area, with an outside bar and posher restaurant inside. Immediately outside the pool area there were mini-golf and tennis courts, but it was all slightly derelict. Following some lush green paths away from the pool there was a sort of jetty, with some rickety boats which clearly had seen better days. It led onto an arm of the Guayas river, but the tide was usually low, and all the eye could see was a swampy muddy surface where some adventurous crabs dared to defy the vultures hunting for a quick lunch.

We adapted to our new environment very quickly. There were no cooking facilities, so we had to have all our meals at the club restaurant, which my mother found a godsend – she is that odd combination of an excellent cook who absolutely hates cooking. The staff knew us quite well by then, because we were the only ones who had breakfast there every day. It was nothing fancy, eggs, ham, bread, juices and coffee. And the Ecuadorian speciality we refused to try because it looked weird: cut and mashed fried plantain or large bananas. We started out by having juice every morning, either fresh pineapple or melon. It was clearly made from freshly cut fruit, but there was an after taste to it which took us some time to pinpoint: onions. We concluded that whoever sliced the fruit in the morning hadn't washed the knives properly. The taste wasn't always there, but we turned it into a sort of gambling game and made bets on our daily juice order.

When the time came to get us enrolled in a new school, we accompanied my father to the Colegio Sulamericano, a flashier than average high school which was not far from the apartment he had leased for us. Its main building was a grand old house surrounded by trees, and we could see there were new classrooms built all around it. I think our visit was on a normal school day because I remember some kids eyeing us up. We met the headmaster, a stern looking older lady with buck teeth like Freddie Mercury and glasses which made her eyes look huge. We weren't charmed by her or the school, but the decision had been made and that was where we were going to spend part of our days for the next 2 years.

I'd always assumed it would be easy for us to adapt to studying in Spanish, because it is very similar to Portuguese. But once I had to actually attend school and follow lessons I found it hard. Some words were misleading, they were the same but meant totally different things. We carried on living at the sports club for about a month, while waiting for our stuff to arrive from Brazil. We were getting quite attached to that place, with afternoon dips in the pool and playing around riding the massive Galapagos turtles which the club management kept as pets. My dad got us both push bikes, so we could cycle around the club perimeter. They were fancy, American made with a light frame, like a racing bike. I'd be too wary to cycle outside the club gates, but my sister was happy to explore the whole area beyond it.

As we learned later, the whole of Guayaquil had been built on top of a swamp, technically speaking. It was more like soft sediment resting on hard rocks. Whenever big trucks drove past outside I could feel the ground shaking a bit. At first it was a bit disorienting, but we were reassured it was normal and no homes would crumble down because of it. The city was also prone to earthquakes and tsunamis, but luckily, we only experienced one earthquake – more on which later. It was permanently warm, but it didn't have the variety of the temperate/ subtropical climate we were used to. Between January and April, it was hot and humid, and it rained a lot. My father was persuaded to rent the upper floor of a house, just in case the ground floor got flooded during the rainy season. All houses in Guayaquil had full window netting inside, and a weird venetian blind sort of system whereby individual slats or plastic panels could be wound open or shut on the outside. This was because apart from the floods, *guayaquileños*[7] also expected swarms of locusts to invade the city for a few days during the rainy season. This was not the seven plagues of the Pharaoh, but it did put us off the place for a while.

Before we moved on to our new home we had a few adventures at the sports club. One of which was the time my sister set off on her bike, along with one of the Ecuadorian junior officers, to explore the wildlife around the club. She was amazed to see a sort of lunar landscape, with dry craters and cracks on the ground, not too far away from our main hub. She decided to park the bike and have a look around on foot. A few steps later she found herself submerging through the cracks, which were hard on the surface only; beneath it was the soft sediment on which the city stood. She looked around and started to panic when she noticed huge crabs poking

---

[7] People born in Guayaquil.

out of some of the distant cracks, and some not so distant ones. She yelled for help and luckily the junior officer, having realised she had not been cycling behind him, was making his way back. He pulled her out and brought her back, covered in light grey mud. I think she made a bit of a drama out of it for maximum impact, but then again, I might have done the same in her place. On another occasion, we were getting up early for school and my sister – it always happened to her! – was in the bathroom when I heard a scream and saw how she got out of her school uniform faster than lightning. It turns out there was a scorpion in her pocket. We both freaked out and ran off to find my dad, whose room was nearby. There was a slight infestation of scorpions in that place, which made it harder for us to relax. Luckily the club also had a bowling alley which kept me busy. I'd never been terribly good at sport, or had bowled before, but I really enjoyed it. The whole ethos of the place – and of Guayaquil at large – was US inspired. Middle class Ecuadorian teens got their clothes and accessories from Miami, where most of them spent their summers. Anything to try and avoid the seven plagues of Guayaquil.

We moved to our new home in a neighbourhood called Placeres a few weeks after our incidents with the local topography and wildlife and resumed our school life. To my mind, our new school was interesting and strange. My sister found it dreadful, but I didn't go that far, at least not in the beginning. Or maybe I just didn't want to share her opinion on anything just yet. The school was very different from what we were used to, especially the uniforms. Girls had to wear two-tone shoes and knee length white dresses with two gold buttons at the front, which made us look like nannies, or nurses. Words cannot adequately express how much we hated those shoes, and the entire combo. Although in hindsight, it was more a dislike for me. But I sensed my sister's passionate disgust at what we must wear and partook in it. We were both placed in the same class because she had failed her previous school year in São José. It was a bit strange to be in the same year as her at first, but I soon grew to appreciate it.

I felt a slight sense of superiority as we now were on the same level, even if what I really longed for was to be as welcome amongst the 'in' crowd as she was. Well, I wanted it but didn't want it. Because whenever this actually happened I just ran away from it. A few months into our attendance I developed a massive crush on a boy younger than me, called

Sandro. I never had the courage to speak to him, although he did approach me at the lunch queue once to ask what Brazil was like. We were the object of some interest due to our being the only foreign students at the school, and that somehow bought me some time with Sandro. But I could barely look him in the eye, and spoke the bare minimum, for I didn't know what to say – well, I knew I could never say what I actually felt. I was happy to watch him from a distance. I knew the exact time his class would be down in the courtyard playing football, as it was during my class recess. I would just stand by the bannisters on the second floor, behind a pillar just in case he saw me, looking down as he juggled up a football, sometimes alone, other times surrounded by other clumsier kids. The first time I saw him doing that it felt like an arrow through the heart, like Cupid actually existed. Wounded by beauty. Not that this makes sense either. Perhaps the wounded feeling was the unattainability of it all. At the time I was also reading a lot of romantic novels where nothing ends well and more or less surfed emotionally on that, so it's no surprise that I fed my soul the hopeless sightings of Sandro exhibiting his teenage hormones on warm mid mornings. Because when a real romantic opportunity was presented to me I more or less freaked out: this happened on my next school year, and the exact circumstances escape me; but it was during after-hours activities, when I found myself playing ping pong with a boy I didn't really know, except from a distance during break. He was probably also slightly younger than me, with jet black hair and blue eyes, but he also looked a bit like an Inca Indian. I have no idea how or why we started to play, and how odd it was that the school seemed to be deserted. But I do remember a gradual crescendo of panic on my part – and with the panic, the speed at which I hit the ball also increased. But all he was doing was steer the conversation (or mostly small talk) we were having during the game towards something a bit more romantic. I began to sense what he was doing and started to get nervous, guessing where it was going. He asked things like 'do you like films' and similar, trying to get a sense of what I was like. I felt my face getting redder by the minute, until he said: 'well, now you have an invitation to the cinema'. It was rather a nice way to ask someone out. Not that I saw it that way then. I probably said OK and ran home straight away, never giving the poor boy a definite answer.

I have thought about this event years afterwards, trying to discover why it spooked me so much. All he did was ask me out. It could be that I was much more comfortable with a dream than with reality. Because I did live in a self-constructed dream of sorts at that age. Maybe every teenager is like that, but I had the very distinct impression that was not the case with my sister or others like her. There was another boy in our street, whose brother was a friend of my sister's. His name was Santiago, he was older than me and quite good looking. I didn't know him that well, but I thought he was nice and friendly. Well, one day I felt Santiago was connecting to me in a similar way to the boy from the ping pong game. Again, I had a slight panic about the whole thing even if I did have a bit of a crush on Santiago. To this day I still don't know why I reacted that way, but I was definitely afraid of what intimacy with a boy would be like. I had the desire for it but fear always stopped me. I had never kissed a boy and went through my teenage years a virgin on all counts. So, I preferred watching them from afar, placing my affections on those who would not reciprocate. That brought a lot of heartache during my teens and twenties, but it kept fear at bay.

During our first school year we met a girl who would become our best friend throughout our stay in Ecuador and beyond. Her name was Mariangela, she was tall, with short hair and freckles, sharp witted and very friendly. She became a friend to us both, with no difference of treatment, which to me was a first (Majo excepted). I don't think we got on that well with any of the other girls in class, and there weren't that many boys either. Apart from Mariangela and a couple of other girls, I had the same distant approach to school girls who seemed to be interested in nothing but make up, parties and boys. I didn't seek their company, and nor did they seek mine. It was an agreed arrangement with no big issues on either side. My sister didn't actually care about them either, she perceived them as stuck up dolly girls showing off their latest Miami jewellery every time they came home from holidays.

We were having a bit of trouble following class, though. Spanish wasn't our spoken language, and although it was similar, it was a different story trying to follow books in a language not that familiar to us. I remember one of the first days at class, when I found myself trying to follow a Geography lesson and kind of giving up on it after the droning voice of our teacher nearly put me to sleep. The only time in recent years where I'd heard any spoken Spanish was during our trips to the beach in Brazil. My uncle Wilson would stick a Nat King Cole cassette on, from his Mexican phase, and we'd spend the next 3 hours on a singalong to *El Bodeguero, Las Mañanitas* and a few more of his hits. But this woman had none of Nat King's velvety tones, and I suddenly found myself summoned to the front to answer some questions on the topography of the Andes. I had no idea what she was saying and looked at her and the class, alternating between helplessness and mild panic. She was asking me about the characteristics of a llama and what could I tell the class about it? I was completely out of my depth and one of the kids whispered to me: *tiene tres patas* (it has three legs). I repeated that as in a trance but got finally woken by the laughter. I did know what I'd said just as the words came out of my mouth but had no idea why I'd said it. My father realised school would not be as easy to follow as we all thought and decided on hiring a Spanish language teacher to help get us a bit further and catch up with the other students. And so, me and my sister started to attend private lessons at *Doña* Emilia's home, which was two blocks away from us.

Her house was odd. But then nearly every house I visited in Guayaquil was odd. Our school friend Mariangela's house, for example, looked huge from the outside, but it also looked like it had been built piece by piece, and with no symmetry, like a Lego sculpture. Most neighbourhoods were not very pretty to look at, I think because houses in Guayaquil had to be built to withstand floods, locusts and all the rest, with very little regard to aesthetics. But the streets looked mostly like war zones as well, full of buildings with high pillars where elegant flats hid from view. We went to visit a school friend in one of those places once. This girl's family was supposedly quite wealthy, having made their money off Ecuador's best-known coffee brand, which later in the visit I realised was named after the family's three children's last name syllables put together. Having crossed the hallway downstairs, slightly surprised to see the dump these rich people lived in, we were even more astonished to enter a super modern apartment full of the latest mod cons, and a three storey one at that! I think they even had a swimming pool. It looked like something behind Willy Wonka's many strange doorways. Come to think of it even our school was like that. It was only after many visits to Mariangela's house that we discovered there was a separate basement apartment where her grandmother lived. We were taken down there once to meet her. I found odd how they kept her there hidden away, like some Phantom of the Opera, but it was her own choice. It was like Miss Havisham's lair [8]. She had lots of chintz around and the TV was always on, as she watched South American soaps almost 24/7. Mariangela told us she'd been engaged to Mexican star Cantinflas once, and I did see his framed and signed picture on a mantelpiece, but I suspected the engagement was a figment of her imagination.

Our new Spanish teacher Ms Emilia lived in a house which looked very narrow from the outside, but as soon as we went inside it was obvious that the space itself spread inwards into a rectangular shape. We never stepped beyond her sitting room, but we often saw her sister coming out to make us snacks, and her niece who was always going out somewhere, usually looking glamorous in a Black-Friday-sale kind of way. This was 1979 so the whole BF concept hadn't been invented. I guess what I mean is she always looked very made up and dressed up all in gold lamé single strap leotards tucked into tight jeans, with lots of jewellery and a short crop of peroxide blonde hair to complete the look. Whenever she did stop to talk to us she was always nice and friendly. The mother had the opposite look to the daughter: she always looked like she'd just got out of bed. She usually appeared at the beginning of our lessons to make *llanpigachos* and *patacones* to serve at break, along with tamarind juice. We'd never tried this stuff, and in hindsight it was probably really tasty, a mixture of fried smashed plantains and potato cheesy croquettes. But our lesson usually started after lunch, at around 230pm, so serving us food one hour later would have been a bit much. But we were curious and didn't mean to refuse the kind offer (the former reason was actually more accurate), so we accepted the first time and they just assumed we'd want it every time.

Snack time was a welcome distraction most of the time. Ms Emilia was trying to teach us verb declinations and all sorts of grammar at a time when most people in that city were having their *siesta,* and even if we were kids, we could feel the slumber creeping in as we stewed in her dimly lit sitting room and could only just make out the brightness of the glaring sun outside through the plastic blinds. The gentle but constant rattling sound of the fan didn't help keeping us awake. I could see my sister's eyes

---

[8] Character from Charles Dickens' *Great Expectations*

occasionally drooping down. We had a couple of ways to stay awake: I found Ms Emilia's hair, or rather the lack of it, strangely fascinating. She had black hair which sat on her head like a helmet, but I could see her scalp through it. It was like she had a thin layer of cotton candy over her head, and she sort of back combed it, so it only followed one direction. It was probably dyed black, as she was old enough to be a grandmother. I could spend some time in almost silent admiration of how she managed to cover her entire head with so little hair. She always wore red lipstick and a generous layer of pressed powder, and against the chiaroscuro of the sun outside and the shadows of her living room she reminded me of Vincent Price as Prince Prospero in Masque of The Red Death. The other distraction was a litter of kittens usually taking residence on her big sofa, which faced the table where we sat. The kittens were at the age when they start to explore the world, and even if Ms Emilia would be blind to their shenanigans we were highly amused by them, to the point where we struggled to contain our laughter. She seemed oblivious to anything that did not relate to verb declinations. So many years later I realise how good at teaching she was, and she probably was responsible for getting us through school and giving us the tools to communicate and connect to kids our age in a foreign country.

After about 2 or 3 months of tuition and once we were much more confident with the language, our classes ended in an abrupt way. One day, in the middle of our lesson, the doorbell rang, and two policemen came in and marched straight through to the back of the house. Ms Emilia was confused, and so were we. There was a moment when time seemed to stop, she didn't know what to do and looked at us to check she wasn't imagining things, but she could see we had the same look on our faces. A few moments later we heard a crescendo of noise, some shouting coming in from the back of the house, and in a matter of seconds we saw the policemen escorting Ms Emilia's niece in handcuffs, looking deeply ashamed, followed by her mum screaming for them not to take her daughter away. The three of us just probably sat there open mouthed as this scene developed like a crap whodunit. After they'd gone, her sister was left behind still wailing, and I barely remember how we got out of the house, but it was probably a rushed request from poor Ms Emilia. We never found out if the niece was embroiled in some shady business, and we never went back to their house.

By that stage our handle on the school environment had a tighter grip, we 'd made a few more friends, and felt somewhat comfortable with rules and regulations. But even all of Ms Emilia's efforts could not prevent me from failing my school year. I think I just gave up. It was my very short rebel phase. My father had dragged us all the way to this weird country with its backward society, so I'll teach him a lesson. That was likely the subconscious reasoning for my not giving a damn whether I failed or not, because I'd always been a fairly straight As and Bs student. I knew I was going to fail about 2 months before our final grades were revealed. It was no surprise to me. But I returned home with that doomed piece of paper, and found my father anxiously looking at me, waiting for the verdict. He knew I hadn't been doing well. I told him I'd failed, and he was devastated, which made me feel remorseful. Maybe if I'd tried harder, I might have succeeded. My mother didn't seem to mind one bit, rather she had a more philosophical and practical take on life. I couldn't believe my sister had passed her exams and I hadn't: it was unheard of. I felt the humiliation of returning to the same year, having to get to know my new (younger) classmates, and watching my sister and best friend get ahead. I felt left behind, and it was a feeling that would sit in my heart for years to come.

In the middle of all this, we were slapped with a mandatory participation clause on the official school dance event. We were split into groups according to year, and so I was placed on the folk-dance presentation, whereas my sister and Mariangela got the lucky ticket: jazz dance presentation. We had to buy some fabric and order special dresses from a local seamstress. My dress consisted of a white top joined to a wide layered skirt with flowers on a yellow background – very Frida Kahlo, in hindsight. But peer pressure meant I just felt a bit ridiculous wearing it. I didn't mind the presentation music that much, or the whole event for that matter. But I could see my sister was about to kick up a fuss about the whole thing. All I could think was, 'you're the lucky ones, stop complaining!'. But I didn't say anything, in fact I could yet again see a chance of piggybacking on my sister's rebellion, like I'd done when she refused to board the school bus years before. That didn't end well, but now we were older and maybe our parents would back us. I'm not sure what my sister's goal was. I thought she just wanted to drop out of the dance. I tagged along because I was a bit sick of being a goody-two-shoes. If this was my one-way ticket to teen credibility and independence, I would grab it in a heartbeat.

But the whole affair got resolved in a way that I wasn't expecting; my sister not only managed to get a blessing to drop out of the dance, but to quit that school as well! What! I thought; I got the short end of the stick, not only did I have to shut up and re-join the dance, but I didn't get the option to follow my sister out. I suspect she had been quietly cooking up another solution all along, and if she hadn't, my father was desperate for her to continue her education in any way available. She got enrolled in the American school of Guayaquil, which in my eyes was the absolute triumph, a place where she would be taught in English, not have to wear any dodgy uniforms or two-tone shoes and have some really cool people as teachers. With some trepidation, I asked my parents to allow me to join my sister in the American school, under the justification that I didn't like our school either and why couldn't I get the same treatment? My parents begged me not to make life harder for them as my sister had just done. So, I didn't. But I couldn't believe that the roll of the dice could land me in a permanently losing situation. That's how I thought about those things back then. Years earlier, we'd been playing War, a board game in which you won if you conquered the greatest number of territories. My sister beat me twice and I got so infuriated and angry I locked myself in the bathroom, crying with rage and frustration, getting even more upset as I heard her and my dad laughing outside, telling me not to take it all so seriously. But I did take most things very seriously, which made me quiet, analytical and scared, for most of my teenage years. It took me a lot of work to eventually lift up that veil.

But before she kicked off her latest rebellion and left the Colegio Sulamericano, we had quite an earth-shattering experience for the first time in our lives. It literally shook the ground we stood on. The whole of the Andes territory is prone to earthquakes, and we had heard of it before arriving. My father had met the Chilean attaché in Guayaquil, who told him his apartment block had to be built on specially engineered conditions to withstand the frequent earthquakes. Chile is located along a vertical strip across the Andes, and they were used to them. For us it was an absolute fright. I remember exactly where I was and what was happening. My classroom was on the ground floor facing the courtyard, and none of the other classrooms had glass windows, only open rectangles looking out. We were passing some papers forward to the front when I felt the ground rocking upwards a bit – but as Guayaquil was built on soft clay, all it took for the ground to shake any day was a heavy truck driving by. But then a second motion started, and it was horizontal: one moment I could see the wall next to me, next moment it had moved to the left and back again. But what I could never forget was the noise, like a primeval rumble coming from the depths of Mordor. It made me look up at the sky and think of God, something I hadn't attempted even during my first communion. If any thoughts did cross my mind it would have been something like to ask God if my time was up and if it was I hadn't had that much to live yet.

But luckily, we were on the ground floor and all the other students seemed to know how these things went. We all went outside and waited for the rumble to end. I could see groups of girls huddled together crying. I also saw my sister, who'd just come down from her classroom, and to my surprise she was crying. I had been a bit spooked at first but now I was almost laughing. Why were these people crying? It was obviously over, and it seemed comical to me. My sister didn't appreciate my reaction. When the earthquake started her Physics teacher, Mr Ramírez, simply rushed out, getting kids out of his way as if they were inconvenient obstacles. Once it was all over his credibility plunged to zero and my sister was clearly shocked to discover her teacher was an absolute coward. We saw some senior school people come out of the main building to assess if there had been any structural damage to the school. We were slowly ushered to the main gates because there could be another tremor imminently, not that I was really expecting it to happen; at that stage nobody knew what to expect. By the school gates we saw hapless and worried parents beginning to arrive, shouting out their children's names to make sure they were safe. At a distance I could see my father approaching, his white navy uniform and cap visible amongst other parents rushing towards the school. He was on foot and told us how it happened back at his work, which had offices at a tall-ish building. It was scarier to be on upper floors, as the quake motion would have made the building highly unsafe. My father told us later – with a degree of mockery – how the women were screaming their heads off and everyone on a mad scram trying to rush downstairs. Back home, we found most of the bookshelves collapsed and a fair amount of mess everywhere.

My mother told us how our pet dog, Maria Benedicta, started barking and crying out minutes before they heard the quake roaring. She said she tried to go downstairs but her hand could not physically hold the bannister because it kept moving out of reach. All in all, we had survived with no major scratches. I think it was one of the most interesting experiences I had at that age.

There was another experience which wasn't so interesting or even pleasant. I think it happened when we hadn't been in Guayaquil long, but Mariangela and I were already good friends. We normally walked to school because we both lived a couple of blocks away in opposite directions. We had been walking out of the school until the junction where we split ways, and we noticed a man in a small pick-up truck drive past us slowly and smile. We thought this was a bit odd - and said our goodbyes. I carried on for another block or so, and I remember it was a hot day and I felt the glare of the sun zigzag across my eyes as lunchtime traffic built up. Suddenly I felt the pick-up truck we'd seen earlier driving slowly next to me, and I stopped, thinking he wanted to ask for directions. It stopped as well, and as I looked through the passenger window I saw a man smiling and not saying anything. He kept smiling and then he looked down, which is when I noticed what to me looked like an upright sausage emerging from his trousers. It took me a split second to realize what was happening. I looked at him again and he was still smiling, with the dumb expectation most flashers hold towards young girls. I stood there for longer than I should have, wondering what he expected me to do next. I had no experience of such people, or of ever having seen a real penis. I once found my father's Playboy magazines stashed away and had a look at them, full of curiosity and anticipation for I don't know what. There was only one picture of a naked man on it, and the sight of it confused me greatly. It resembled a forest of hair around two fat fingers. I hadn't been that curious about male genitalia, or any genitalia for that matter. That picture spooked me a bit. And now here I was, standing in front of the real thing, which looked repulsive. Was this sad man really going to be my introduction to the opposite sex?

I rushed away from the car feeling my cheeks burning with shame, fear, and maybe also mortification. I looked behind me but thankfully the car had gone, the flasher content enough with his pathetic climax to leave young girls alone for a while. I hadn't really thought about it until now, but perhaps this episode left me in no rush to encounter a real penis, or sausages, again. I walked back home, still a bit dazed by what had just happened. I laid my school bag on my bed, got ready for lunch and said absolutely nothing to anyone at home. I didn't say anything because the embarrassment would have been too much, and the mention of male genitalia to my parents, and that somehow, I was in on it or the knowledge of it. It wouldn't change the event, it happened, and no one could do anything about it. After lunch the phone rang, and it was my friend Mariangela, who tentatively asked me if I remembered the car that stopped near us before we parted ways. I said yes in a way that told her I knew what she meant but didn't know how. She almost screamed that the same man had exposed himself to her in exactly the same way, and that as she saw him driving away towards me she guessed what would happen but was too dazed herself to reach out and warn me off him. We exchanged impressions, our voices reaching a high pitch of nervousness. My mother could hear us from her office. But I never told her what happened and was grateful to find my best friend had also been prey to her first flasher. It was nice to have company in trauma.

My friendship with Mariangela got stronger after my sister left our school, even if the three of us were still hanging out together outside school hours, but at the Colegio Sulamericano our bond grew. I would visit her home quite often, the strangely built Lego-type house. She was one of four, and untypically for an Ecuadorian family they had mostly Spanish ancestry. Mariangela and her brothers and sister were mostly fair and freckly. Her mum was a tall friendly lady and her dad was freckly and quiet. Her home was always welcome and chaotic, feeling more like an old inn of court than a family home. They had two maids who were obviously of Quechua Indian heritage and seemed to permanently live in their kitchen. Lunch at their home was usually a sort of Cuban style rice and black beans or *menestra* (brown lentils) with *patacones*, the fried plantain addition to any Ecuadorian dish. Study time at Mariangela's was never a simple proposition because it was necessary to deal with the entire family, on top of the strange architecture of that house. It looked a bit like the Weasley's house in the Harry Potter movies.

Our apartment was also a little bit odd. The floors were made of marble looking slate, and all the rooms had at least half of the walls wood panelled. There was a large balcony where we kept our new pet dog Maria Benedicta and two mongrel cats. The dog had been offered to us by a school friend, who was adamant it was a German Shepherd puppy. When we arrived home with it my dad said we'd been conned; that puppy would never be anything other than a mongrel. We didn't care because she was so cute, as all puppies are. She was a strange dog though, never quite creating a true attachment to any of us. She was a bit like a cat in that respect. We'd also rescued two kittens from a shelter, and called them Giraldo and Zabata, inspired by my mother's favourite book about Spanish medieval musicians. Cats and dog became inseparable, after a short period of vicious fighting. Like my mum predicted, we both lost interest in the welfare of all pets, and it was left to the house maids to look after them. My parents had hired Josi, a young black girl just a bit older than us, and Carmela, an older mixed race (Indian and Spanish) cook. I remember that employing domestic help was essentially a benefit to the country's economy. My mother used to say how strange it was that they didn't get on, the mixed-race cook looking down on the black girl. Black people were a bit of a rarity in Ecuador. The only black communities were to be found in the province of Esmeraldas, which was where Josi was from. The majority of the country's ethnic fabric was either Spanish, a mix of Quechua Indian and Spanish, or pure Quechua. The latter were the most derided. My mother employed a young Quechua native boy called Pablo, who came in once a week to wash the balcony and communal areas. She had a soft spot for him, as for most ethnic indigenous minorities. Pablo worked quietly and not very efficiently, and the only time I heard his voice was when he replied to anyone calling him. He had a short bob of raven-black hair and lovely bronze-coloured skin, and from my bedroom window, whilst struggling to stay awake doing my homework, I could sometimes see his black hair shining in the sun as he scrubbed the floors. He was a teenager like us, and I'd sometimes wonder why he wasn't at school or having fun somewhere else. Sometimes I'd spot him looking at us quizzically, as if he did not understand why we were here. My mother would often attend dinner parties hosted by my dad's Navy friends, who were for the most part conservative Ecuadorians. She would return from those events quite shocked at what she had heard said about the indigenous populations, that they were mostly useless and should get jobs like everyone else, or even worse, be exterminated.

We went on a big family holiday to Quito and Cuenca once, after my dad had bought his big imported 1979 Ford Fairmont. We drove all the way to Quito, the Ecuadorian capital which was nested right in the middle of the big Cotopaxi and Cayambe volcanos. The altitude in Quito was much higher than what we were used to at sea level, so we had to move slowly to allow oxygen to the brain. My mother rushed to answer the phone at our hotel and fainted before she reached it. The air was clearer, temperature was cooler and even the people seemed more civilized. There were also a lot more Quechua Indians living there, perhaps because it was nearer to the routes towards the Indian markets on the mountains. I loved the place, it reminded me of my favourite cartoon character Tintin's Temple of The Sun adventure. I found myself thinking, why can't we live here instead? No rainfall or floods, no locusts, no excessive heat…but the chances of earthquakes were higher and so I abandoned that idea.

Our time in Guayaquil led to the next step in my love of film. I'd been a bit fascinated by South American soaps, which played non-stop on Ecuadorian TV, and kept young and old (like Mariangela's grandmother) captivated and entertained. I liked to watch bits of them all, to the absolute astonishment of my sister, who found them horribly kitsch. But they had something that caught the imagination of even the most cynic of spectators: they had the sort of structure that kept people watching, much like when Charles Dickens serialised Oliver Twist. Anything could happen to the characters according to audience reaction and none of it was a done deal. The main producers of soaps were Mexico, Venezuela and Argentina. Brazil also, but I knew plenty about them. Mexican soaps were amazing, with a very clear divide between the evil and good characters, and also rich and poor; they weren't very subtle but still great fun to watch. I remember a soap in which the villain was a middle-aged woman who wore a dress and an eyepatch made of the same flowery fabric! And she was an assassin as well! Venezuelan soaps didn't have a very wide pool of actors, so we'd keep seeing the same people playing similar roles. They were usually seen as the permanent good guys, so God forbid them being cast as villains – it never happened. And most soaps had title tracks by romantic macho singers like Jose Luiz Rodriguez, known as *El Puma* (the puma) for his long face and huge black mullet. Argentinian soaps were a bit different, trying to be a bit hip and modern but still peddling the most outrageous melodrama. Their most famous 80s soap was about a cute orphan girl who was a bit of a Pollyanna. She spent the entire plot searching for her mum, who it turns out was an amnesiac cleaner at the same orphanage.

My sister didn't like soaps, but she liked movies as much as I did. And again, like at the Naval Base in Bahia, we didn't have to go far to find a cinema: around 2 blocks away from us stood the Cine Inca, a standalone cinema which occupied an entire block, even if it only had one screen. We'd go there often with Mariangela, or just the two of us, or I'd go on my own to watch horror flicks, which my sister hated – well, what she actually hated was being scared. This cinema was my big introduction to the world of horror films. It often had double bills during the week, something I hadn't even heard of. This was around the year that Halloween and Friday the 13th were coming out, and I watched them both at Cine Inca – not as a double bill, because newer hits were never scheduled together. So, I'd get to see Halloween as the main movie, and the first one would be something the programmers thought no one would be interested in but they wanted to keep bums on seats until the main attraction started. But I usually loved the trashier selections. I don't know where they got their prints from, but they used to screen old Roger Corman, Hammer horror and APi films, which were three of the best-known genre production outfits. I saw some great Draculas, all starring Christopher Lee. And a very unusual one with Jack Palance. A few of the Quatermass series as well. There would be some occasional rubbish ones, but I just loved the concept of watching two films in one go. There was no candy store at the entrance, but we were allowed to bring drinks, so we normally got a couple of Inca Colas before each screening. Inca Cola was the national soft drink, the Ecuadorian Coke. Coca Cola was sold in Ecuador but not everywhere. It was easier to find Pepsi, but we were suckers for the lime green fizzy taste of Inca Cola. Its bottle had a blue medallion logo imprinted on it, like an ancient Indiana Jones god or icon, or a relic you might find in Machu Pichu. Sometimes there would be a hot dog vendor outside, and at the break I'd pop out to get hot dogs with onion sauce to go with our drinks.

Around the time our movie going hit its climax, the second instalment of Star Wars, The Empire Strikes Back, was on general release. I hadn't been such a huge fan of the first film, unlike my sister, but I enjoyed it enough to tag along for the sequel. I actually had big doubts about my sister's taste in film, after her obsession over Tony Manero and Saturday Night Fever, so I wasn't expecting much. But I was *enthralled* by Empire Strikes Back, and I've watched it many times since, trying to find out what caught my imagination so intensely at the age of 15. It's a finely crafted movie, almost old fashioned in its linear narrative, but so full of real characters and inspiring images. I didn't know I'd become a film director then, but in hindsight I was admiring seamless direction. My sister was also completely under the film's spell. All in all, we watched it 7 times, all of them at the Inca, almost within an entire week. She took a camera and a recording device because she wanted to keep the memory of it eternally, along with the massive crush she had on Mark Hammill. She recorded some of the dialogue on my mother's portable cassette player, mostly the scenes in which Luke Skywalker is being taught by Yoda. Over the next months, she'd play that non-stop, sometimes speaking the dialogue along with the actors. She also photographed Luke's big close ups which took most of the screen. She tried to do it with a flash a couple of times, and only got away with it because at 230pm most of Guayaquil was having their *siesta*. I thought we'd surely get thrown out of the cinema, but no one came for us, not even the projectionist, who was probably napping as well. A double bill would take us from around 2pm to 6pm or more, and my parents were pretty relaxed about it as long as we'd done our homework. I was always pragmatic about doing school work, but my sister cared quite a lot less about it or about keeping our parents sweet.

My sister's new school seemed to be very lenient in terms of homework: she never seemed to have any! Meanwhile I was stewing in my own spite and trying to ignore any titbits relating to new teachers or students. But she seemed to be a lot more relaxed and at ease since changing schools, so I couldn't stew much longer. The four of us went to her school a couple of times, when they had American holiday celebrations like 4th of July. It was quite small and didn't feel like a school at all, kids wearing their normal clothes and teachers being young and hip, unlike the stern planks who taught me at *Colegio Sulamericano*. I am probably being unkind and unforgiving, but I'm trying to describe them as I felt it then. My parents were relieved to see my sister at least happy about being in education. They feared her imminent defection from any hierarchical institution she felt was imposed on her. But she seemed happy enough, even if later on when we moved back to Brazil we discovered her American school diploma was worth peanuts within the Brazilian education system. That was a blow to them, and it pretty much made my sister give up on school for good, to my father's despair. My parents had been brought up with the notion that education is the only way to achieve success in life, so they feared the worst for her. But at that present moment no one knew what was coming. They were so happy about her contentment they even allowed her to join the school trip to the Ecuadorian jungle later in the year.

Our fascination with other cultures and countries continued. We had visited the mountain towns and Indian markets by now, amazed at the different lives those people led. Quechua Indians were usually small in stature, even the men. Most of them had lovely silky complexion and shiny black hair, like our young scrubber Pablo. Both women and men wore felt hats, and sometimes also their kids. Their market stalls were full of handicrafts and handwoven woollen ponchos and jumpers, with beautiful designs and intricate patterns. These places were also usually full of foreign tourists, and for me and my sister it was an incredible opportunity to practice English.

Earlier in the year we'd been hanging out with a lot of American sailors, although I can't quite remember how that came about. Likely it was their visit to the Naval Club, which we also continued to enjoy at weekends. Suddenly there was a sharp increase in American voices around the swimming pool, and we knew something was afoot. My dad mentioned there were three USS ships stationed at Guayaquil port and so we set about trying to break into their society. Well, my sister did, and I followed, as usual. They were only around for a few days, but I remembered those days for a long time afterwards. They were polite young men who were welcomed into our home and met our parents. I think they weren't expecting to have family-oriented time off, but I was sure they welcomed it, being away from home for such a long period of time. I remember two privates, Andy Wilkinson and Ed Kooning – amazing how I still remember them perfectly. Andy later sent us photos of himself cleaning his rifle, which I didn't understand. He seemed quite sweet, why would he need a rifle? It was likely an introduction to NRA Midwest culture. I've always had photographic memory for names, faces and events, which can be a curse and a blessing – I would have a very hard time writing a book of memoirs if I didn't, but it also means that I can access a memory bank I never knew was backed up. My teenage years were fraught with mostly wonder, pain and confusion, like everyone else's, I imagine. Thinking about the American sailors I still can't elicit what that felt like, only distant echoes. There was one young man I hung out with most, and that was Ed Kooning. These guys would have been in their early twenties whereas we were 15 and 17. Ed Kooning and a couple of other sailors came over for dinner and hung out with us for the next 2 or 3 days before their ship departed again. We didn't do very much, apart from spending time with other kids in the neighbourhood and play bowls at the Naval club. But Ed Kooning remained in my memory for a long time afterwards because it was probably the first time I felt totally understood and appreciated by not only a boy but actually a MAN. It was the first crush I had on someone which was reciprocated also on a deeper level. That's what I was left with after he was gone. Nothing romantic happened between us, because I think Ed felt I was unprepared for any level of intimacy at fifteen, and maybe he was also just a sensitive soul who would not engage with the 'girl in every port' cliché. At that age I was entirely unaware of any impact I might have on the opposite sex. I still felt a bit like a child and in truth scared of entering the adult world. Ed Kooning was my safe passage into it, or more accurately, introduction to it. Weeks later I received a letter from him, which I still have somewhere, thanking me for making his time in Guayaquil the most special of his entire journey at sea. His letter made me realise I had just had a taster of what falling in love might feel like, being with someone who didn't require me to be anything that I was not. I had touched his heart, and he had touched mine.

On this same year we also travelled to Europe for the first time. We had been to the US the year before, on a Christmas visit to my mother's childhood friend Madalena, who lived in Miami, Florida, with her Greek husband Demis and daughter Atlanta. It was our first time in the US, and we loved it. I could finally place the scent of the McAllisters' home at the Naval base, it was everywhere we went. It was inside the envelopes of Ed Kooning's letters. I never quite smelled anything like it, it was a mixture of freshly ground past, future and linen together. In Miami we set out to visit Disney World with Atlanta, who was a similar age to us and spoke a delightful broken Portuguese. I don't remember much about this trip apart from the camaraderie between my mother and Madalena, and the strangely quiet streets surrounding her house, full of mock Spanish colonial houses like theirs. By then I hadn't realised Americans moved around mostly by car, and they didn't hang around street corners like our neighbours in Guayaquil. On New Year's Day my father could no longer bear the absolute silence of suburbia and stepped outside to yell 'happy new year' to any residents still nursing a headache or tucked up in their beds. Nobody came out or yelled anything back at him. We enjoyed our last few days of holiday in the same quiet manner, but this was our first proper introduction to American life.

When my mother suggested we take a month's English course abroad to expand our horizons, our first thoughts were to go back to the US, which we had loved so much. But she had another idea in mind: why not go to England instead? We would have a more cultured experience and learn things not easily available in the Americas. I didn't oppose this because it piqued my curiosity, and my sister had the same reaction. It was arranged that we would be with a travel agent the entire time, who would place us with trusted British families throughout our stay, not in London but in a smaller more manageable town. And so, we set off for Littlehampton, by the coast in the south of England. It was February 1980 and I had never experienced cold weather like it. None of the coats I had brought were enough to keep me warm. I was initially placed with an elderly couple at a lovely big house. They lived with the wife's sister, also elderly. The first night I spent there was like being in a museum, or at a parlour stuck in time. I remember their sitting room at night, all of us having digestive biscuits with tea and watching Spoils of War on Granada TV. Tea was served with milk which I initially refused. I couldn't have wished for a more sudden immersion in British culture. I wanted a glass of water but came back from the kitchen puzzled at not seeing where their filter was. The old biddies laughed their heads off, wondering which terrible jungle I had sprung from, where there were obviously no taps? I explained we never drank water from the tap because it wasn't clean, and they were even more amused by this. I had a nice chintzy room where everything was covered in floral fabrics, and they let me have a small heater. They were very nice and clearly in need of company, but I found it boring.

I'd heard my sister's accommodation had 2 dogs and 2 more lodgers, so I campaigned to be moved to her house. It was certainly a much more frazzled household, but also more fun. It was dreadfully cold in our room though, so cold I could see my own breath. The entire house was freezing, except for the kitchen diner, which was kept permanently warm by an old Aga stove. I started to miss my luxury room at the old people's house, but it was too late, and I didn't want to make a fuss. The landlady was Janet, a nice no-nonsense woman, who ran the household with her husband Des. They had a disabled son a bit younger than us, who had been deprived of oxygen as a baby, had some paralysis and needed full time care. I think a house full of students was a good way to keep his mind busy, and he did have a sharp mind, he loved talking to us. The other lodgers in the house were 2 young Scottish lads called Angus and Steve, who were attending some sort of apprenticeship scheme. At home we had been accustomed to helping ourselves to plates of food at meals, whereas in England you would get your plate served up and that was it. I found it mean at first. One of the Scots boys saw me leave a chicken breast almost untouched on my plate (it was totally tasteless) and asked if he could have it. I nodded and was shocked to see four hands grab the piece of chicken off my plate – they were fighting for it! I'd never encountered hunger before, but this was also clearly a cultural chasm of some proportion. I reasoned that either people in England didn't get enough to eat, or us in South America wasted food on a daily basis. I think the latter was actually true.

Every day we got the bus at the same stop, and it was thrilling to get onto those red double-deckers. I loved the English streets, with their brick houses and manicured gardens, so far away from the chaos of life I had grown up in. There was a young man who always got the same bus as us, he always wore a black leather jacket and had blonde peroxide hair. He was probably a follower of the punk movement, which I knew zilch about. I was intrigued by how someone with such a distinctive look could just sit on a bus next to an old grandmother with pearls and a blue rinse and no one would bat an eyelid. This sort of detail increased my fascination with this country of contrasts. I was glad my mother had made us come to England instead of the US, which no longer held much interest to me. It was a short stay, but it planted a seed in my mind that grew as the years followed.

When it was time to leave, I think we took a taxi to Heathrow – I don't remember how we got there, but once we tried to check in my sister discovered we weren't booked on the flight departing in 2 hours. I had no idea how to deal with this new challenge; we were 2 teenagers left to their own devices in a foreign country – we had no idea what had become of the travel agent who was leading our group. We didn't have any money left, and the next available flight would leave in one day. I was getting hungry and put some pressure on my sister to resolve the situation. Luckily my mother had written lots of emergency contacts on our travel diary. She eventually found the number for my aunt's sister-in-law's *sister*, who was living in London at the time. She told us to get on a cab and head to her home in St John's Wood. She paid for the cab when we arrived, fed us and put us up for the night. Much later on they got a frantic call from my parents, who were panicking because we hadn't arrived on the flight we were supposed to. We made it back safely, although on arrival, I don't know how but both of us had contracted scarlet fever AND nits. Three weeks were spent in bed, on antibiotics, wearing plastic shower caps with anti-nits powdered meds. My parents wouldn't let us travel on our own like that ever again.

But England was the country where I saw Sam Peckinpah's Straw Dogs for the first time. Our language school had a film club where they regularly screened films past their general release. I don't think they operated any sort of rating or stopped minors from seeing any films. I was 15 when I saw it, and it left an impression on me, not just for the violence but for the visual mastery. I had seen violent films at the age of 9, so it did not affect me much. I could see something beyond it, in the case of filmmakers who were real artists. Truth is, I didn't exactly know what was going on in Straw Dogs, and I even had a slight awareness I really shouldn't be watching it at my age. But it was another film that burned into my retina.

Many years later I was honoured to have worked with David Warner, who played the 'village idiot' Henry, but was too shy to ask him about Peckinpah. And not long ago during a trip to Cornwall where the film is set, me and my husband Jack took a detour back to London via St Buryan, the sleepy village where the opening of the film takes place. I was amazed to see that almost nothing had changed in over 35 years, the triangle of churchyard, pub and corner shop looked frozen in time. Back in 1980 I had little awareness of time and how long it would take me to return to this strange and wonderful place where rain and milky tea were a constant.

Back to Ecuador, and Brazil after a few months. We had to give our dog away as there was no way it could have come with us, but fortunately one of the neighbours wanted it. Our young maid Josi wanted to join us in Brazil and my mother helped get her papers in order. Our older cook, Carmela, was more than a bit jealous. But she was a complicated woman, if endowed with a wicked sense of humour. She had an easy banter with my father, who loved to tell crap jokes she always laughed at, so they established an interesting rapport. Most of the time she was in cloud cuckoo land, telling us tales about a fiancée from Cuba who was coming to marry her and set up home anytime soon. She had a job at a tinned tuna factory before she worked as a cook and used to tell us conspiracy theory stories about how we shouldn't touch Ecuadorian tinned tuna because it was produced by the CIA to poison the population or some even more outlandish tale. When our dog was taken away, she declared: 'the small dog is gone but the big dog stays'. She spoke in riddles sometimes. There was no way my father was going to take responsibility for her in Brazil, so she did indeed stay behind.

We had to stay at my grandmother's house for a while again, as my parents had given up the big apartment we had before leaving São José. But it seemed that my sister had settled down a bit in her latent teenage rebellion – apart from the fact she had attempted to do a runner again before we left Ecuador, because she didn't want to come back. This time I played Judas and grassed her up, a bit sick of witnessing this cursed merry-go-round. She wouldn't have been allowed to return of her own free will anyway – not from a country a few thousand miles away. I thought I'd done everyone an act of charity. But she had mellowed out and our stay at my grandmother was not fraught like before. This time we were not about to find a new apartment again, but in transit to our next destination: Brasilia DF, the federal district, the new capital of Brazil since 1960s. Rio de Janeiro had been the Imperial capital since 1820s, when the Portuguese king took refuge to escape Napoleon's troops in Lisbon. Then in 1956 the new president Kubitschek decided to build a new city right in the centre of Brazil, to decentralize economic movement from the huge Brazilian coast and establish inland activity. When my father heard about the new posting I couldn't understand why the Navy would send him to a place with no ocean in sight for hundreds of miles. But his new job would be more about teaching naval strategy and it was promised to him that after two years he would get a permanent post in São José. This was a big boost to my mother, who had to do her PhD from abroad, and also had to turn down job offers in academia, but such was the life of a military wife.

When we were very young, and my mother worked as a teacher at a school well known for its communist diktat, she would be invited, or even goaded to attend protests and marches against the government. This would have been not long after the military coup in 1964. She always told us, much later, about the feeling of unease she had when the headmaster herself instructed the teachers to spy on students, to check if they were right-leaning themselves or if they came from conservative families. She refused to join a protest once, because of us — she didn't want to run the risk of something happening and her daughters becoming orphans. My father had warned her that if she ended up in jail because of those protests he would not come to her rescue. But my mother was never a commie, she just felt deeply for the indigenous communities she became friends with during her PhD research. She understood why people become attracted to socialist causes, but her experience at the school left her in two minds about the sincerity of any political cause.

Brasilia was a strange place, even if we had a happy period there. I was at the end of my teens and my sister was in proper adult mode already. We were given a huge military apartment with more rooms than we needed. It had a massive living room, almost the size of a tennis court, with faux colonial fittings which my mother hated, but we couldn't redecorate just for a two-year stay. Young Josi had come with us and was delighted to see new places and new faces. My father had to yet again face the unfortunate event of a parent dying while he was in transit, this time his mother, my grandma Edith. I hadn't seen or heard from her in over two years whilst we were away, and I must confess I wasn't even a bit affected by her passing. I was still young and perhaps harbouring an eternal grudge against her for not holding me in the same high esteem as my sister. Or maybe I was just preoccupied with having to adapt to a new school all over again.

My sister had had her comeuppance before we left São José, when again she was placed at a pretty forward thinking and expensive school owned by my aunt's sister-in-law, a towering domineering lady named Zelda. All my cousins had studied at that school and it was meant to be the bee's knees in education standards. But it was very demanding and fostered a competitive mentality among its students. I think she had to be transferred to another forward-thinking private school, but by then the damage had been done. Her time at the American school did not get an equivalent diploma in Brazil for some obscure legal reason, and so she faced having to repeat a whole year in order to carry on her studies. She didn't much care for school anyway, so she decided to ditch the whole thing, which probably broke my parents' hearts for a while. This time I could understand her dilemma though; I might have done the same myself, and I was secretly relieved I didn't get my wish to transfer to the American school back in Guayaquil. I couldn't have faced repeating 2 years at school. Not that I was that bothered about my studies either, but I could feel my father had placed his last hopes of seeing one of his daughters graduate on me. And dropping out would never have occurred to me because the necessity of acquiring a degree had been drummed onto me from an early age, so I just carried on.

While writing this chapter about our stay in Brasilia I got talking to my sister about it because I simply could not remember what she did there for 2 years. I knew she'd dropped out of school, but then what? I received a text message from her: "I smoked dope, rode my bike, explored parks and aqueducts, ate mushrooms, wrote, drew, suffered, loved, drank, did everything except study". It reminded me that I didn't know her life at all. She walked into the lift with a friend once, who asked about sharing a spliff. I knew what marijuana was but had never tried it. I wouldn't have even considered trying it, based on my parents' scaremongering stories about it being the gateway to a descent into drug hell. Like a tabloid headline. But on that day, I felt my eyes turn like saucers to my sister, as if asking a silent question. She noticed the shock in my face and tried to dispel it, but at that point I was still taking anything my parents said as gospel. She must have felt alien to us most of the time. We didn't hang out together much, because by that time I had sourced my own friends and suddenly come into my own person a bit more.

There was one time when we did go out together, with one of her friends, for a drink at one of the bars on the next block. I was on a mission, having failed one of my exams and needing a bit of relief from it all. I thought I could maybe join into my sisters' lifestyle. I ended up drinking the equivalent to half a bottle of *cachaça* (infamous Brazilian sugar cane spirit) mixed in *caipirinhas*. I had never drunk in my life, maybe a beer or a glass of wine here and there. I had to be carried home afterwards and couldn't remember any of it. Except for a thought flash as my bottom scraped the grass as we moved, and someone from the bar ran after us with one of my discarded shoes. I couldn't remember getting home, only waking up the next day with my mother sleeping on the floor next to my bed. I felt dreadful and couldn't tell anyone why. I had to be taken to hospital for glucose injections, and for years after I couldn't bear the smell of lemon juice and alcohol. Days later my sister told me I'd started insulting everyone in the bar, including some people we knew. I had blacked out completely. It was to be many years before I drank any alcohol again. But the worst thing about it was that my parents blamed my sister for what had happened. They didn't make a big deal out of it, but the inference was that I'd been taken off the righteous path by her influence. At that point in my life the mantle of *goody-two-shoes* was starting to weigh on me, but it was the injustice of such judgement that bothered me. I did protest - a bit - but by that time my sister's legend had been cast.

I had been enrolled at the Albert Einstein school for my final two years, a promisingly named but sadly not glitteringly genius-like institution. I found the school a bit odd, especially because of the diversity of the student body. I had never been in a classroom with so many kids from different parts of Brazil, or whose parents were not from Brasilia itself. This being 1982, no one born in Brasilia could have been older than maybe 20, because the city itself had been officially founded in 1960. My classmates were literally from every state in Brazil except my own. There were regional differences in their speech and behaviour, such that I learned a lot about my country during those two years. I'd heard that people from Minas Gerais were usually crafty, cautious and good negotiators, which I found to be mostly true. But I saw a whole other side to them, which was great fun. And being the snob that I was — some would say am -, I thought them to be mostly devoid of any sophistication. Brasilia being a new city, there was no great culture hub, or even much interest for it. It was a matter-of-fact society, built for practicality.

We lived in a sort of square made of various housing blocks, and this was a model which repeated itself like a fractal throughout the city. It had been purposefully designed to engineer a certain type of social interaction. Each square normally had a small park or grassy area in the middle of it, and squares were connected by the artery of a small commercial street with shops like bars, markets and grocery stores. We didn't have far to go to get basic shopping done because it was in the master plan. Seen from above, the city looked like a 2D sketch of an airplane, with housing squares located either on the north or south wing. Those were for the middle class. Further out from the wings were the north and south lakes, artificially constructed because Central Brazil had no natural water, and surrounded by grand houses, which were mostly for the wealthy, government ministers and high-ranking civil servants. Everything in this city had been artificially constructed, even the suburbs, called satellite-towns. They quickly became the poorer areas, with menial labourers working on both wings and lakes and getting back home to satellite-towns, which started to grow like fungi beyond what the architect Niemeyer had predicted.

Our housing block was mainly for Navy officers and their families. My father had been posted to Brasilia on a teaching position, which he enjoyed greatly. Whenever we had low grades on subjects we weren't that keen on, which were primarily physics or maths, my father would sit with us and make sure we understood what vectors were or how the pi number behaved. I would be amazed at his excitement about numbers and symbols which were an annoying mystery to me. The only time his excitement became contagious to me was when he was giving me support lessons on electricity, because I had developed a crush on our supply Physics teacher. His name was Alfredo and he drove a baby blue VW Beetle. I knew that because I had stalked him out of the building to find out if he had a significant other. I mapped out the only route he could drive through from the school one day, and at lunch time I rushed ahead and hid behind some bushes, waiting. Soon enough I heard the splutter of his car and could see a baby blue shape moving beyond the trees. I started walking as if I hadn't seen him coming and heard a beep behind me. Alfredo was offering me a lift and my cunning plan had worked. It was a half-baked plan though, as I had no idea what I would do if he fell for my charms, or how exactly to put those charms into practice. I was seventeen, still a virgin and had not even had a snog yet. So, he just gave me a lift to a place that had no use for my journey back, we had a chat and I thanked him. It was a pretty pathetic result, but I had butterflies in my tummy. I was happy to just bask in his attentions. I dressed better on days he taught us, and my classmates started to spread the rumour I fancied a teacher. I didn't tell anyone, and they probably didn't find out, but I suspect Alfredo did, in which case he was very good about it, being friendly but not overtly so. In any case, thanks to my crush on him I managed to get the highest Physics grades I ever achieved in my school history. My father thought he'd been the cause of it, and I never told him the truth.

I got used to the new school pretty quickly, also because I knew it would be my last. It wasn't a very inspiring school, but then none of them were – except for the school with tap dancing nuns. But this place was meant to catapult my will towards higher education, and it wasn't doing that. On my second year there, I barely made it through the chemistry and biology classes. Even history and languages, usually my favourite subjects, were taught by a couple of robots just happy to repeat information. None of the new teachers provoked any hint of a crush on me, so I couldn't use that particular momentum to get me past the finishing line. But by then I was unaware I'd been following my sister's gospel and choosing seats further to the back of the room, usually joined by my new best friends Lydia and Xarope.

Lydia Weber – her full name – was a bit of a firecracker, the daughter of a pianist who was friends with my mother. Her mother was a statuesque German violin player who'd divorced Lydia's father years earlier, setting up a new home with another pianist. Lydia had been raised in a strong musical culture and was a cellist herself. She was around my age, and we had been introduced by our parents, who more or less expected us to become friends. But we sniffed each other suspiciously like dogs, both thinking we weren't going to befriend the other just because our parents wished it. At school, I ended up in the same class as her, and little by little we approached each other after recognising we had a lot in common, mostly an absurd sense of humour, a love of books and a restless intelligence. We got on like a house on fire, and she soon joined me at the back of the room, where we spent the more sleep-inducing classes composing literary riddles which kept us highly amused. My other friend Xarope (childhood nickname for Roberta) would eventually join us on a more regular basis, even though she cared a lot more about her grades than myself or Lydia, who had zero concerns about flunking school. Sometimes I wondered why she was in school. She had no interest in academia and was being groomed to be a professional cellist anyway, so she relished in absolutely ignoring everything the teachers said and charming their socks off while doing that.

I was fascinated by her zest and her beauty. She had inherited her mother's looks, blonde, slim with blue eyes, but with an easy manner and a warm personality. She looked like one of the Mean Girls, except she wasn't mean at all. She befriended everyone and was always smiling. I guess I was also a bit jealous of her; how could someone so gorgeous be so nice? Not even a hint of a bitch? I'd notice the admiring glances the boys threw her, but she seemed oblivious. Or just not interested. Because at that time she'd also developed a crush on another Physics teacher called Jair. He wasn't good looking, in fact he looked like an upright sheep with a blonde poodle perm, but he made up for it in brightness and charisma. His classes were the exception to our freeze regime, and I could actually learn from the way he taught us. Lydia engineered things so that he agreed to teach us both privately at my house, as support tuition. After one of the lessons I was to approach him privately to tell him she liked him, when she gave me the signal and went to the toilet. I think the poor man was caught unawares and not expecting it at all, or at least if he suspected anything he never thought we'd be so bold as to come out with it. To his credit he gently explained how inappropriate it would be for him to reciprocate her feelings. It would have been easy for him to take advantage of this beautiful 17-year-old girl, but he didn't. She was upset, but I respected him even more after that.

Roberta had been nicknamed Xarope for some time but not even she knew why. She was sharp as a razor, very bright and funny. Like me, she looked more geeky than gorgeous, and probably harboured a similar slight jealousy towards Lydia. But it was good natured, because we really enjoyed each other's company. Xarope was one of 4 kids, the eldest girl with 3 younger brothers, from a family originally from Minas Gerais. She was also into music and had been a piano player since a very young age.

What struck me most about her was her no-nonsense attitude and her habit of telling the truth even if it got her into trouble. For a while the 3 of us did everything together, and it was exhilarating to find kindred souls in the prologue to my adult years. I gave me relief, actually, from all the time I felt alone in my early teens. I no longer needed to hang around my sister and her friends to find peer contact. I think we naturally grew apart a little during this time, not that we meant to. She was hanging out with some people I considered "normal", and also with others who were a little more of a challenging nature. But gone were the days when I would avoid the weird ones like the plague; I took them as they came, and my sister seemed happy enough.

My main cinematic experience in 1982 was watching Spielberg's ET on a big screen with Xarope. I still remember the mall we went to, and what time of day it was. It was such a powerful film to watch at 17 years old (or any age really), such that I have no recollection of any other films I saw in Brasilia, and I'm sure I saw many others. I have watched it again many times since, but I never cease to marvel at it. I find it a miraculous film, everything about it has a touch of magic, as if the filmmaker was channelling some higher vibration or intelligence. That's not to say I don't have huge admiration for Spielberg: I do and have admired many of his films since. But I have come to believe that such powerful messages, be it in art or entertainment or music, are transmissions received by inspiration. That extended scene [SPOILER ALERT] where ET comes back to life gets me every time, but at a deeper level as I grow old.

Back then I wasn't thinking that I would eventually like to do the same job as Spielberg, but there was definitely a sense of my destiny and creative pursuits being entangled. I think it was around that same year that I got a letter from one of Brazil's best known and loved poets, Carlos Drummond de Andrade. I had written to him asking for any advice for budding writers (me). Because I'd spent the first half of my entire life buried in books, the desire to write them myself grew stronger each day. The day that letter arrived, I jumped around the house, full of joy and pride: he had replied to ME! And it was a monogrammed two-sided postcard filled with his spidery handwriting, just like I'd seen on my literature books! His advice was simple: read, read, read, write, write, write, and repeat. I have no idea what I wrote on my letter to him, but his words made me hope I had a future as a writer. The only writing I had done so far were the riddles and tales I wrote with Lydia and Xarope, apart from the handcrafted paper I had published within our family circle. I started to sketch short stories and poems as well, not really sure what I'd do with them.

The final school years were proving to be tougher than I'd thought. I was so completely uninspired by it I just wanted it to end. I was aware of my father's anxiety about my graduation. He kept asking if it was all fine, and I guess I had to tell him not all was in fact fine. There were a couple of subjects I couldn't – or wouldn't – get my head around, it was a bit of a rebellious thing because I was sure that, had the teachers been better, I would have learned a lot more. So, I stubbornly lumped all the blame on them, until I realised that attitude would get me nowhere. Well, that wasn't technically true because failing would land me in a lot of trouble. I made a herculean effort to get the minimum grades to pass, and I did, which made my father very happy. He didn't care how low my grades were as long as I could move along to the next stage of my education.

In my defence, I had a lot of distractions at the square where we lived. The building next to us belonged to the American Embassy, so a lot of their lower attachés were living there. I had flashes of the McAllisters all over again, but this time I could actually speak English. There were some chairs outside the main entrance where people usually congregated, it was a meeting point of sorts, mostly for the kids. We got to meet some of them, slowly at first. They seemed a bit suspicious or even wary of non-Americans. There were 2 brothers, Christian and Craig, who had the run of the place. They were a bit younger than me but were zesty as hell. They made us chase them around the whole grassy area for a whole afternoon, before granting us even a hello. Xarope started this game, intent on meeting Christian, the youngest and cutest (according to her). From that moment on he ran away whenever he saw her. But we got quite friendly and I had a bit of a crush on him, even if I thought it was a bit tacky to like someone younger. I had seemingly got over the Sandro effect, but maybe not completely. I also got on well with a younger girl called Bertha, who rang our buzzer nearly every day after school. I'd come downstairs to 'hang out' as the Americans called it. Whenever I had Lydia round for homework or coffee, she turned her nose at the American kids a bit, calling them morons. I think she got a bit jealous of my all-hours friendship with them or couldn't understand why I was hanging out with younger kids. I often asked myself that question and felt a degree of shame about it. I don't know why, because apart from Lydia no one had a go at me for the age gap in my friendships. I was fond of those kids, but if I was to psychoanalyze myself at 17, there were veiled reasons why. My fascination with anything or anyone foreign, and perhaps in hindsight a sense that my future did not lie in my own country. I felt at ease with Americans and people from other cultures. The other, shadier reason was to do with the discomfort in my soul that told me I had not lived my early teens properly, had not had the experiences others had, and this was a way to live vicariously through them.

My sister was hanging out with some local punks, essentially rich kids whose parents were diplomats and who'd just come back from a posting in England. They wore their rebellion in the shape of a torn T shirt full of safety pins and snarls rehearsed to a tee. But in the middle of Brazil, in a city full of civil servants and families minding their own business, their battle cry was more of a yelp. They formed their own bands but finally realised Brasilia was a cul-de-sac for post punk sounds and eventually moved to the coastal cultural axis years later. Some of them became quite famous and still play the lucrative 80s revival gig circuit. In 1982, they simply kicked their nascent anger around the city's squares, not really outraging anyone. One of them came to a house party me and my sister hosted, to which I'd also invited most of the American kids, Lydia and Xarope. My parents had retired to their room, leaving us young people to have some harmless healthy fun. It started out like that, but heaven knows why I decided to put a sign by the lift downstairs telling people to come up to the party at ____. I honestly thought I was being helpful, but the apartment filled up with people we'd never seen before. Punk boy called his friends, who arrived with beers and other substances my folks would have vetoed, had they known about it. Soon enough the punks were picking fights with the older American red necks – one of them was a Texan with a confederate flag above his bed – and things came to a halt when punk boy smashed a beer bottle on a table and threatened one of the Americans, who actually wasn't a red neck. They raised their voices high enough to attract my parents back in the living room. The party was declared over, with no major war wounds inflicted on anyone. It was more likely a case of too much drink at a young age, like me and my forgotten insults at the bar.

Before I finished school, one of my major crushes was on a boy called Jairo, who wasn't in my class but was the same age as me, for a change! Same year classes were split in humanities and sciences, which meant we had a lighter workload of the opposite subjects. I never really spoke to Jairo because of my shyness and feeling of total inadequacy. His nickname was Goblin, which was probably due to his small height and strong body, like a weightlifter. He was blonde with a short crop, with blue eyes and a mouth full of teeth which almost projected outward when he smiled. By that description it's not entirely clear why I found him so attractive, but I did. Soon enough my classmates sniffed my preference and teased me relentlessly. Goblin himself probably knew I fancied him, but we never spoke. But I was happy to just watch him at break or at sports day, slowly realising that for the first time my body knew what lust felt like. By this stage I hadn't discovered John Hughes films, but once I watched Pretty in Pink or Some Kind of Wonderful, I felt those films had been aimed directly at me as an audience and wondered how a grown-up man could so perfectly relate and recreate the teen feelings of non-reciprocated desire.

Our school had a couple of big events, a gymkhana with no horses but with lots of teams with different tasks to perform, cultural and athletic. There was a prize at the end of it, a weekend trip to a famous mineral baths resort, with natural warm pools, woods and wildlife. Our team actually won the prize in the end, but I dropped out of the trip. I didn't feel connected to the other classmates, didn't want to spend days with them, and more importantly did not want anyone to see me in a bikini or bathing suit. I had developed a high degree of criticism towards my own body shape and felt confronted and vulnerable when I had to display my teenage body to people I didn't know. There was nothing wrong with it, except the picture of it on my mind. Fortunately, I never had eating disorders, just the perennial presence of scales and diets. But it had an impact, it stopped me accepting invitations to friends' pool parties or beach holidays. There wouldn't have been that much peer pressure or media messages blasting images of the ideal body shape and I can't put my finger on how exactly that distortion took shape in my mind, but that's water under the bridge.

I am yet to be fully cured of that affliction – someone once said it's called body dysmorphia and most women have it.

The other big event was a Brazilian national holiday called June Feast, taking place at the end of June. It coincided with the holy days of St Anthony, St John and St Peter. In case I haven't mentioned it, the Catholic faith is the absolute majority in Brazil, although as I write in 2018, various evangelical faiths, with pastors in the vein of Billy Graham, have become increasingly popular everywhere in the country. Every time I travel back to see family I notice new churches sprouting everywhere. Back in the 80s we hadn't heard of this denomination. But June Feasts were mostly great fun, and since I'd been a small child we always had school June celebrations, in which we had to dress up as 'country' people, or as its stereotype... Straw hats, flowery dresses, pigtails, cartoonish make up – I wonder how actual country dwellers never complained about this coarse characterization. End of June was usually still winter, so any feast would have a wooden fire in the middle of it, with various stalls selling caramelised apples, corn snacks, warm chestnuts, mulled drinks, sweets and bonbons. One of the most popular services was called Elegant Post, which was basically a Valentine's courier, except it wasn't St Valentine's day, but since St Anthony was the patron saint of lovestruck people, it was said that he gave lovers a little helping hand by delivering messages throughout the whole feast duration. He was there in spirit, of course, because we did most of the hard work.

I was recruited as one of the Elegant Post couriers that June and was wondering whether to overcome my boring shyness and maybe send Goblin a small note. That thought came to me as I was returning to the main stalls area from my latest delivery, and I was determined to act on it. Fate, however, had other plans. Within my field of vision, the party continued on, but like a time lapse there stood in the middle of the square my crush, Goblin, facing another girl I didn't know, very close. He had his hands around her waist and hers were around his neck. Only they seemed to exist in that moment, and although he had his back to me, I could see the look of love in her eyes. It seemed to happen in slow motion, but they kissed and stayed in that spell for a long while. I remember the scene like a shock, as if it was suspended emotion in my heart, like I could not feel the discomfort, but I knew it was coming. I don't know how long I stood there, probably long enough to make sure I wasn't imagining things. Phew, what if I had sent him a note? I would have scrambled egg all over my face, for the shame of it, to become vulnerable and expose myself and direct my affections where they were unwanted. For me these events elicited high drama, but mostly in my head. I never shared it with anyone, but just collected the shattered pieces of my vanity and tried to quieten my heart until things turned out the way I wanted. Thing is, I wasn't really sure what it was that I wanted if I did get the boy I liked. I hadn't done a lot of progress in the romance department since the Ecuador days. It wasn't like I had zero success. Even the young American kid, Christian, who'd started dating a pretty girl from our block, was giving me signs that he'd much rather hang out with me instead. We had a slow dance at a party at the American consulate, but I think my pride told me it would look bad to go out with a younger boy, especially one shorter than me.

One of my sister's friends had a slightly bohemian lifestyle, was a piano player and hung out at our house a lot. He was a lot older than us, studying law at university, but music was his real passion. Him and my mother had a lot in common and they used to spend hours in her office doing piano improvisations together. My sister and I suspected they both had crushes on each other, but it was never confirmed – to me anyway. My mother came from a generation when women would not fool around, but she was a sensitive soul and this young man was like a kindred spirit in the way my father could never be. I actually asked her, many years later, if she'd ever fallen in love with other men and she did not deny it. It was a platonic crush, which fed their inspiration and had no business manifesting in matter. This young man, Silvio, had a friend who would sometimes turn up out of the blue with a flute, and join them in their improvs. I cannot remember his name, but he had a dreamy air about him. He was also older than us, doing a music degree, and had started to turn up more regularly. My sister told me it was because of me, but I ignored her – it couldn't be true. But it was, and he did eventually speak to me in a matter of fact way, such that it took me some time to realise what he was getting at. He thought I was cute, enjoyed my company and why not see where that would take us? I also thought he was cute, even if I didn't have any major crush on him, but to me that was an invitation into the unknown and that scared me quite a bit. I know there is a paradox here: not being sure what I wanted with a boy didn't stop me lusting before, so what was different? Probably the fact that in this case I could not control the outcome as I could not control the trigger of it.

I graduated from school with no major psychological scars, but I had to really stretch myself to not let my father down. I could tell he was anxious about my results, and I managed to just about scrape past the finish line. He was happy enough because I now qualified for the massive pre-university test called Vestibular, which I decided to do in Brasilia even though we were about to move back to São José. I figured it would be easier to pass a Fine Art degree test at a less prestigious university and I could transfer it to the one I actually wanted to attend as they were both state universities.

Truth is I wasn't entirely sure of what I wanted to do with my life, but Art was a damn fine way to find out. We had a comfortable middle-class life and I didn't have to work as long as I was in education – even if it had to cease at some point. I went into the exam room with some trepidation. The maths, chemistry and physics parts were challenging and made me wonder how on earth I'd managed to graduate. I put all my chips in the humanities, and especially the bonus writing challenge which was worth loads of points. When I got the results, that was my saving grace. I'd written such a highly graded story it pretty much made up for all the zeros on other subjects. It was obvious I was never planning on being a mathematician or some such, so they got me past the hurdle with approval on my chosen subject. My father was ecstatic, and with that we began preparations for our return to São José. Which went not without trouble, because my sister was inspired to run away again in protest as she wanted to remain in Brasilia. At 19 though, her misguided rebelling found no agreement anywhere. I think she was old enough to actually decide for herself, even if my father still had some hope she would come back with us and continue her studies. But she was also old enough to realise life on her own without the cushy room, the nice apartment and ongoing parental support would be hard indeed.

We didn't have to stay at my grandmother's this time, because my recently deceased paternal grandma had left us an apartment in the south area of São José which was big enough for us all. And my father was finally free to stay and work in São José, no more postings abroad or to other parts of Brazil. My mother was glad about that, but she felt it had come too late for her career to take off. She'd got her PhD in Ethnomusicology but found out she was too qualified to be hired in Academia at that time. That did not fill me with confidence for a similar path for myself. I thought the return to my home city would recalibrate my path, but the truth is I felt a bit adrift at first. We thought transferring my place at the Arts degree from Brasilia would be a doddle, but it wasn't. In fact, I could not transfer it to any other university, which meant I found myself in a similar predicament to my sister years earlier. I'd have to sit another exam in a year's time if I really wanted a higher education.

The prospect of university called to me, because basically it HAD to be more inspiring than school was. At least I could pick the subjects I wanted to pursue. I took it on and enrolled in a booster course to refresh my memory bank and clarify what I'd never really understood. I had applied to a prestigious higher education institution, the University of São José. I really wanted to go to their Fine Art faculty but had read somewhere it was the most in demand course out of the humanities. I didn't think I was disciplined enough to study until I dropped, or maybe I didn't want it badly enough. I tried for Literature, English being my first option, followed by French and German. I also applied to study History at a private university, but I'd still need to sit an exam. To my surprise I was approved for the Literature degree, although not my first option, but I thought French would be fun as well.

When I sat my History test it started well enough and I felt I could pass it without much effort. But one of the staff assistants came to speak to me and asked me to step outside. She told me I'd been seen trying to cheat and look at others' papers. I was outraged, especially because I was completely innocent of such charges. I'll admit I had cheated at school years earlier, but it had never crossed my mind to repeat that behaviour now. I thought back to a few moments previously when I was thinking about the answer to a question in my mind, and my vacant look was directed by chance to one of the desks nearer. They saw that and assumed I was trying to read someone else's answers. I denied and protested, but they didn't believe me, and I was sent home and my application annulled. I didn't mourn the loss of a career as a historian, but I was humiliated, nevertheless. People in class guessed what had happened and gave me shameful looks, assuming I was guilty. Perhaps it was fate intervening because I would have wasted my time going for a subject I really liked, but with zero inspiration as to how it would have served me.

I embarked on the French Literature degree with great momentum and also pride. It wasn't easy to get a place at this university. It was one of the best and also free to attend. My parents were very happy, and I thought I'd hit the jackpot – for them. I was pleased about it but had a nagging doubt about what on earth I would do with such a degree. It turns out my knowledge of the French language wasn't as advanced as it needed to be in order to follow the highly specialised study of the great French writers. I enjoyed it immensely to start with, as I felt pushed to learn and to improve, and I had no problem doing it within a subject that interested me. We were studying Guy de Maupassant's short stories, all in French, and my lack of knowledge was making me sweat a bit. I had an issue with the French language teacher, a fat Japanese woman who'd obviously forgot where she placed her sense of humour. I'd never met a fat Japanese before and that, coupled with her sour face, kept me distracted from paying attention or even striving to learn anything. The other subject which I found fascinating was Linguistics. And, again, the teacher was another woman who'd had a comedy bypass. She looked angry all the time, even as she was explaining some amazing theory on how words are born. So, my two favourite subjects were taken over by a couple of wet blankets. Now Latin, which was my LEAST favourite subject, was surprisingly taught by an old-fashioned professor who looked like he lived in the 1950s, but who clearly loved his job. And he communicated that love through his teaching. I loved his classes and I grew to love Latin as well, gradually learning to appreciate and stand in awe of a 'dead' language which had influenced so much of how we organise our thoughts.

By now I had inherited my father's Brasilia, a little second-hand car he'd bought in its city namesake. It was a VW, Brazilian designed and made, compact but sturdy and cheap to run as well. I learned how to drive in this little wonder, my father teaching me the basics of clutch and accelerator action all around São José's hilly streets. When it was time to sit my driving exam I passed first time. I needed a car to drive to University every day, so it worked as a gift for my new driver's license as well. But I had begun to slack a bit. Despite the Latin classes I was beginning to feel trapped in a degree which offered no real prospects after graduation. I was sure I wasn't cut out to be a teacher. I'd originally chosen the course because I loved reading and writing, but surely, I was allowed to become a writer without the need to graduate in Literature? The thought of a future spent writing papers on whether Flaubert's Emma Bovary had a secret desire to be a housewife after all just filled me with dread. This dread must have slowly filtered into my daily resolve to drive to class early morning and instead of going in I'd decide to move to the back seat and have a nap until a more interesting class came along in the schedule. By the middle of the semester I was doing that regularly. My grades started to drop. I was considering dropping out, but my mother stepped in with a less radical solution: I could 'lock' my course and take a sabbatical, a sort of gap six months to a year, and decide what to do later. We both fobbed each other off, me by agreeing with her plan, her by thinking I just needed a break and would come back to it eventually.

It was around this time that I had my accident. I had just turned 19 and was still wondering what to do with my life. I couldn't make a career out of reading and day dreaming. I loved movies, but the possibility of making them had not even crossed my mind yet, probably because I would have dismissed it as impossible. Brazil had no film industry, except during the 1950s and a few odd releases in the 1970s. TV was huge, especially soaps, but I wasn't interested in cheap melodrama. I was in the middle of my sabbatical from university, the September days had a hanging mist which meant winter was still in the air, and I had the flu. During the night I woke up to go to the toilet but on the way back I blacked out and woke up with my parents trying to raise me from the floor. I felt sleepy and dazed and just wanted to go back to bed, but my mother told me I'd cut my chin slightly and we should head to A&E. I didn't think it was necessary but there was no discussion. I didn't see the damage, but it turns out it was a massive cut, they had to bring in a surgeon to stitch it. Later on, my mother told me she could see my chin bone but didn't want to scare me. After that was done, we thought we could go home, but the surgeon told us I'd need to have an X-ray to make sure I didn't have any broken bones in my face. Turns out I did. Not broken, but a fractured jaw, on both sides. Off I went again to an operating theatre, where my jaw was realigned, and teeth wired together to keep it still. I couldn't open my mouth for the next 40 days. I was lucky to have an overbite, the surgeon said, because otherwise they'd have to remove or break a tooth, so I could eat through a straw.

I don't recommend it as a weight loss method, but fracturing my jaw made me lose lots of weight, because I could only ingest liquids. It was really hard for the first few weeks, but my mother and our then maid, Nice, were always trying to invent recipes they could put in a blender for me. I could even drink steak juice when I got desperate for real beef. Melted ice cream was a treat as well. Or eggs poached under 3 minutes. People felt sorry for me, so they brought presents, treats, my aunt took me to the cinema once – after the swelling in my face disappeared and I stopped looking like a balloon. My mother offered me a special present and what would I like to make up for the hard times? I don't know why, but I chose a drum kit. She had put a certain amount of pressure on me and my sister to learn an instrument, partly because she was a concert pianist, but my grandma had also forced her to learn the piano when she was a toddler and she probably thought she was doing us a favour. I had entertained the idea of learning to play the cello, which I loved. My mother found me a teacher, but the first lesson, the entire 60 minutes, was spent teaching me how to hold the bow. 'At this rate I'll be playing cello when I'm 99' I thought, and so my enthusiasm evaporated. Back in Brasilia I had participated in some music festivals learning how to play percussion, which delivered much more instant gratification, even if it did take me many days to master the paradiddle (the alternate double movement with drum sticks on a snare drum, like when there is a suspenseful announcement). It was a bit like learning to ride a bicycle, and once learned it was never forgotten.

I thought a drumkit would perhaps open the way to something that I actually wanted to do with my life. I was never outrageously passionate about playing music, but I enjoyed it enough to think there could be a career ahead. After I had my surgical braces removed, we went to a music shop and I picked a rather tacky, bright red transparent drumkit which looked like various upside-down Jell-O flans. I started to have private lessons with a percussionist friend of my mother's, but it took practice to coordinate hands, arms and feet playing at the same time. The first time I managed it felt like an absolute victory, and I thought all else would follow. I set up my first band with my sister and one of her friends. I called it the Ephemeral Perennials, against the wishes of the other two, who thought it was two bookish. We only wrote one song, narrating how my accident had happened. I wrote the lyrics and my sister came up with the music. I don't think her friend ever contributed anything, but the band only lasted about a month, so it was a taster of what we could do.

Actually, my sister's friend did eventually contribute greatly to the continuation of my music career: she knew a guy who was looking for a drummer for his new band. Contact was made, and off I went to meet them. I took my sister along to break the ice, because back then I still thought of myself as very shy and lacking in social skills. We drove to a huge house in one of the most glittering of São José neighbourhoods. I met them at the garage of a big fancy house, where they rehearsed. My worries of inadequacy were unfounded, because they were more interested in getting to know me than my sister. They were João the band leader, Rita the bass player (whose mum's house this was), and Wurm the guitarist. We had a brief chat about what they were looking for and set up an initial rehearsal just to see if we could parlay musically. I was just starting out and probably wasn't very good, but they liked my Mo Tucker vibe. I only found out who that was after I joined the band and realised they were big Velvet Underground fans. Mo Tucker was their minimalist female drummer; I wasn't sure whether to be flattered or offended at the suggestion my drumming skills were 'minimal', but this was the first time I felt appreciated and understood by people my own age. Such was the start of my epic contribution to São José post-punk sounds.

The new band was called 400B, not as a reference to anything sexual, but to Truffaut's obscure 1950s film *Les Quatre Cents Coups*. I didn't know anything about avant-garde French cinema, but João, previously a hard-left agitator, film student and pamphlet maker, had plenty of knowledge and references to share. Many years later, already living in London, I got tickets to a Nouvelle Vague season at the National Film Theatre (now Bfi) because I wanted to see the film which had inspired our band name. I was aware of the main French auteurs' highly irregular output, and I'd seen real gems like Godard's *Breathless* and *Band A Part,* and *Numéro Deux* was one of his more challenging works. It was a leftie manifesto, in his own words about "the pornography of politics and the politics of pornography". It was the only film that ever made me mortified to be in a movie theatre. It was pornographic but not porn. People were leaving the cinema one after the other, feeling they were the butt of a joke. A film supposedly made for cult intellectuals with the more likely aim to annoy them. But Truffaut's *Les Quatre Cents Coups* had the sort of affectionate nostalgia I never expected from someone like João. Later I thought I shouldn't have been so surprised because João was someone who liked to throw convention to the wind and defy people's expectations of him.

I was already disappearing into movie theatres, sometimes going to see a film every day at the local mall. Afternoon shows were cheaper, so I'd spend my allowance purely on cinema tickets. I once had a marathon movie week with titles like Francis Coppola's *Rumble Fish* and *Outsiders*, plus *Revenge of the Jedi*, the latest in the Star Wars series, and the first Indiana Jones. I was inspired by big movies, where story, acting and the pure craft of keeping people in a trance for 2 hours were the overall aim, but I did appreciate small brainy films like the ones João loved. My dull university lessons were like a sour memory, even if I knew I'd have to face my mother's expectations at some point and either restart my degree or ditch the course for good. But as I settled into meetings and rehearsals with this merry band of drifters, I felt like I was entering a new stage of my life, where my opinion and output actually mattered.

Chapter 3

ON BEING A
YOUNG ADULT

I wasn't a great drummer, perhaps because in my subconscious I knew I wasn't in this for the long run. I could play pretty well, but I hated drum solos and couldn't be bothered to practice for very long. The beats I came up with were more like statements glued to João's lyrics and Rita and Wurm's tunes. Pamphleteering rhythm of sorts. I couldn't really survive on jam sessions outside the unit I chose to be in, but that was true for the four of us. Wurm was probably the most naturally gifted musician of us all and that rarest of things, a soulful guitarist. He was gentle and quiet, tall and thin with short corkscrew hair and huge demented blue eyes. His real name was Carlos Pacce and like João he was a part time journalist. I never knew the reason for his alias, but it was meant to be a remnant of his childhood. He also drank a lot, more than any of the other musicians I met during my time as a cult/minor pop star. João was more disciplined with substance abuse, but there was also a deranged element to his personality. I'd probably rate him as the most intelligent person I ever met, but with an intelligence which bordered on madness or psychopathy sometimes. People like him can see things very clearly, whereas the rest of the world can't. I could actually be describing a psychopath, but in my mind, I would compare him to the Ray Milland character on the B movie sci-fi classic *The Man with the X Ray Eyes*. Milland's character, Dr Xavier, discovers a formula that gives him the ability to see through things, but he eventually starts to see through all of life and can't bear it. I used to wonder how lonely it must feel, to be able to see so much when most people are blind.

João wouldn't have imagined himself as I just pictured him; he wrote amazing lyrics and his performance was a bit erratic. I'd never seen anyone act onstage like he did, and I wouldn't even say that I liked it, but it was exciting and different. Wurm would play very still and mysteriously, whereas Rita liked making eye contact with us. Our first gig as a foursome was at the underground São José club called Devil's Blue Dress, at an old Italian central district. Everything about this city was Italian born or inspired, so that wasn't saying much. The first time I was at Devil's Blue Dress I really felt I was leaving my whole past behind me and entering new territory. The club was at an old turn of the century house with high ceilings and some dereliction setting in. I've seen bars in Berlin which look similar to how that place was. The ground floor was a bar with tables and chairs for the more bohemian punters, and downstairs there was a basement and dance floor with a stage where bands performed.

I don't remember which band I saw there on my first time, but it would have been someone we knew personally, as all of us rock and pop musicians were or became friends fairly quickly. It felt as if we swam against the current of samba and traditional music, of sun and laughter and carnival, and we were the antithesis of all that. It was a naïve and snobbish assumption, but it did make us happy for a while. I thought that place was the most outrageous defiance of conventional entertainment I'd ever seen. It was owned and run by two brothers, one of whom had dropped out of seminary school. But on club nights he dressed almost like a priest, and religious symbols were strewn everywhere. There was a small cage hanging from the ceiling like a chandelier, and on and off there would be a woman in there, dressed in an ocelot print leotard wearing a Marilyn wig. She'd sit there, peeling off leaves of a white cabbage and slowly eating them, all the time staring at punters in a menacing manner. Devil's Blue Dress was a stable of underground music for a few years as I started to play nights and become a 'night creature' like my three band mates. They clearly had more experience at it than me, and I was looked after and cared for like a mascot.

Devil's Blue Dress also hosted one of our first gigs, our introduction - so to speak - to the underground post punk movement, not that I knew it at the time. My personal style had changed an awful lot since joining the band; I'd chopped off my long curly dark blonde hair to a shorter crop, in keeping with 80s fashion. I dressed in black with check black and white trousers, with faux silver jewellery. But I was glad to be at the back of the stage, hiding behind my drumkit, because my crippling shyness hadn't gone anywhere. I was introduced to other bands, all friends of João or Wurm, and we got other gigs scheduled at other clubs because that's how it was done, you had to know the right people. We had a couple of gigs in Brasilia and smaller cities around São José but playing anywhere other than big cities was a bit pointless. No one knew or was interested in the type of music we played.

To be perfectly honest I had no idea what type of music I was interested in that matched the band's aesthetics. I had been a huge Queen fan in my mid-teens and had even managed to see them live in São José in 1981. I went to the band's hotel with my sister and briefly saw Roger Taylor, who I had a drummers' crush on. I was gutted because he made an escape before I could get an autograph. Before Queen it was Duran Duran, partly to do with my infatuation with anything British, but what also grabbed me was that band's drummer. Also called Roger Taylor. But João and Wurm showed me there was more beyond big pop bands. Gang of Four. Talking Heads. I particularly liked listening to drummers, not because of solos which I hated, but the ones which weaved their beats so beautifully into the fabric of the music itself. I started to appreciate drum solos the first time I heard Ginger Baker playing. And some jazz drummers later. By which time I had drifted away from music as a career.

There were some challenging times, especially when we had a gig scheduled and Wurm had been drinking for three days before. Me and Rita had to go to his apartment to find him completely passed out, next to his forlorn-looking girlfriend. She'd tried sticking a safety pin on his bum, but it didn't wake him. She promised us she'd get him there on time, and she did. But he spent the first 2 songs playing all the wrong notes, standing still with his guitar, but I could see him edging back and forth like a streetlamp in the wind. Behind my drums I could see some green goo dribbling from his lips. João stormed off stage, furiously throwing the mike at the audience. I didn't know what to do, so I threw my drum sticks at the audience as well, trying to make it look like a staged performance. Rita looked at me puzzled and followed us backstage, holding on to her very expensive Rickenbacker bass. João was having a hissy fit, blaming Wurm for his childish escape into alcohol whenever his 'issues' came up. I didn't know these guys so well, even after a year. I sensed Wurm was haunted by something, but I never found out what it was. There was no other way to explain why such a gifted musician would self-sabotage whenever there was a chance of success. João wasn't having any of that, he ended the band that night and asked me and Rita to join his new band, which he had been setting up without any of us knowing. We declined, he was furious, and went on to add our refusal to his new band's name. My time with 400B was not very long, but it cemented a lifelong friendship between us. João went on writing about music and film, and Rita eventually joined his new band. Wurm also formed a new band and seemed happy and more settled. He died years later, after remission from cancer and a heart attack the day he was released from hospital. I think he was a sensitive soul not fit for this world, or maybe his work here was done? That's how I choose to think about talented people who die young. I didn't know what I'd do next, but I didn't feel as lost as I had done in my teens. I felt empowered in my quest for artistic expression.

I had been harassing my father to finance a new trip to England again, and the fallout from the band was the perfect occasion. I set out for the South again, this time a small town near Brighton called Eastbourne. My knowledge of English was much better and taking a language course was just my excuse for leaving. But I did attend classes, even if my mind was much more attuned to what was going on in British society. This being 1985, there was a lot going on. The house where I was staying had a couple of other students, Swiss and Japanese. I arrived at the beginning of February and remember my new landlord Will Harris picking me up from the bus station. It was absolutely freezing, and I'd forgotten how that felt. But Will and his wife Sarah had the heating on in the house, unlike our previous landlords back in Littlehampton. The house was cosy, they had 2 kids who kept to themselves and I was sharing a room with a Swiss girl called Steph, who had big hair, big glasses and big shoulder pads. She was nice to me but complained about everything in the house, things being unclean, crap food, poor lunch bags, etc. I agreed with her on the food issue. This was before the UK joined the EU and Brits wouldn't have known a tasty meal if it punched them in the face. Getting a real coffee was out of the question, it was mostly granulated Kenco with creamer or UHT milk. The house was pretty clean as far as I was concerned, but Steph was Swiss after all. She was just like my grandmother, who would not start cooking until everything had been bleached twice. I suspect she just did not appreciate English culture or life style, she was there to learn English and nothing more. The Japanese girl smiled a lot and said very little.

We would get pack lunches every morning after breakfast, which consisted of a sandwich (usually cheese and ham), a bag of crisps, an apple and a Kit Kat. Lunch for us in Brazil was considered to be the main food intake of the day and I had to adjust my perception a bit. Our main meal would be cooked in the evening, usually early-ish like 630pm. Sarah cooked English classics like roast beef, peas and chips, and everything in between. Steph was right, it was absolutely tasteless or out of a freezer. I wondered where these people got their nutrition from. But this was what they knew, and I was determined to become a Brit for the time I was there. There was something endlessly fascinating about the paradox of the British. Even if I felt I didn't need English language classes I still stuck to them, and I'm sure I learned more through repetition. Eastbourne was the perfect size place for students, with enough leisure and shops to stop us fleeing to London. I used to go out to pubs and clubs with some other students from South America, and this is how I got to meet some actual English people. I found that in general they weren't very forward or friendly, unless they had a drink or two. And this is how I met John Styles, my first ever 'boyfriend'.

I was sitting with some other girls at the local pub and I don't know how but a group of young men came over to sit with us. There was a palpable gaggle of excitement from both sides, even if the way they approached was a bit too assured. Not that any of us minded. I found myself sat next to John, and at some point, he put his arm around my shoulders without asking. If I think back to it and if it happened now these guys would be candidates for a bit of #metoo shaming, because their whole demeanour was that of someone who is claiming a prize. But those were different times, and I started to feel the excitement of having scored a goal: here was a handsome guy, older than me, clearly interested and acting accordingly. Would I finally enter the exclusive club of sexually experienced girls? The answer was yes. I had never even kissed anyone before my second trip to

England. Before meeting John I'd had a semi snog with some guy at a club, after a dance in which I couldn't tell who the most inexperienced kisser was, me or him with his sad mint chewing gum trying to erase the taste of cigarettes and shandy. I was starting to wonder if this romance business was worth fretting about.

I'm mentioning John as my first 'boyfriend', but he wasn't even that. We went out a few times, had a few kisses, and he took me to his house, which he shared with his dad. It was a cold and sad place, with an old man who was almost a shadow in a corner of the front room, like something Orwell might have written about. John took me out for a drive that night, to the middle of some woodland, and if I hadn't been so naïve, I wouldn't have thought it such a great idea. But nothing much happened, except I lost my virginity that night, in the back seat of his car. I told him I'd never done this before, and he was surprised. He said, 'most girls wouldn't have said anything and turned up pregnant next'. I think I said I wasn't most girls. The event itself was deeply unremarkable and a little painful, but nothing I couldn't deal with. After that I only saw him a couple of times, and when I met him at the pub again he was sat with his friends and completely ignored me the whole night. I sat in that pub for ages, at another table, waiting for him to come and speak to me but he didn't. I just didn't get why he would do that, and that's how innocent I was in the ways of romance. I was hurt and upset and started to write him a note on the back of beermats, but I heard some old men sniggering next to me, maybe realising what was going on. I was embarrassed and decided to leave. I eventually found his home again and left him the note I wrote. When I saw him again at the pub he spoke to me, not apologetically but matter of fact, saying he wasn't avoiding me. Maybe he did tell the truth and in my tunnel vision I imagined relationships went a certain way but by then I'd lost interest and I don't think I saw him again. Besides, there was a young butcher giving me the eye on my way back from class, and he sent a message via my landlady Sarah to ask me on a date. Off I went with young Patrick, probably for a drink, but I ended up giving him a hand job. Not that I had a clue how to do that, but I was a fast learner…even if prompts of "don't stop" weren't much to go by. The most interesting part of my initiation into the particulars of sex was the observation of how men approached the whole business from a purely physical perspective whereas

I was this soppy girl lost in a world of emotion. But I'd achieved my main goal: not to leave England still a virgin.

At the end of my allotted time I was in a mind to stay on, because I'd been allowed to attend art school as a guest student after my course was finished. I had been circling the orbit of Fine Art forever it seemed, but this placement showed me there was more to it than just painting and drawing. I found myself in a mildly chaotic environment, in a room full of young Brits who would dress in the arty style of the day, taught by a man who looked like a cross between the Mad Hatter and *Slade*'s Noddy Holder. He also played in a band, like every art person did in those days, and I was invited to see his gig at the weekend. I thought the music was shit, but it helped me bond with my new friends. The girls dressed like early years Madonna or Siouxsie Sioux, whereas the boys were more Mod rockers lookalikes. I'd never seen or gravitated near anything like it and didn't want it to end. I begged my father to extend his financial good will for another month, and naively thought the Harrises were quite happy to have me stay for nothing. They were keen on my staying, but for a price, obviously. Which I couldn't meet, and that was a wake-up call. At the age of 20, it occurred to me that I would have to support myself at some point, because until then my father had been picking up the bill.

I returned to São José with an even greater desire to spend more time in England. Was it an infatuation or the beginning of a love affair? I didn't know, but it hardly mattered. I couldn't do it anyway, not until I got a university degree of some sort to keep my father happy. That wasn't the only reason to go back to my studies though. I truly thought I would need a degree at some point in the future and this was the time to do it. I would have to postpone my dream until the conditions were ripe for another attempt. But until then I had learned how to solve a couple of important issues; I had to tell my mother there was no way I would go back to my Literature course at USJ. I knew it would be a waste of time, but she didn't take it very well. In her mind all I would have to do is go back for 2 years and presto! I would have a diploma issued by one of the most prestigious higher education institutions in Brazil. I think she secretly hoped I would choose a career in academia, but that was almost the opposite of what I wanted.

The other issue was what to do from now on. The few weeks I spent at the art college gave me clarity to choose my next step, which was a return to the arts. I decided to apply for a place at a private university which held similar courses to the one at Eastbourne Art School, but for that I would need to again refresh my general knowledge and sit another exam in a few months. My father approved of this plan, to my relief. He was happy to pay my fees, as long as I stuck to it. I must have been determined to such an extent that I passed almost with straight As and started my degree in September 1986. The course was Graphic and Industrial Design, two subjects into one which split apart after the first year. The school itself was located in an old roman style building, with a majestic entrance decked with hundreds of coloured stained-glass tiles which projected their dancing hues on the imponent stairwells, especially when the afternoon sun shone through, mixed with reflections of passing cars outside. The art studios and photography dark rooms were upstairs, large and looking a bit like concrete bunkers. The atmosphere wasn't the same as Eastbourne, especially where the students were concerned. I felt most of my peers had a style chasm, but that could have been my snobbish judgmental attitude. Most of them were from well-to-do families, whereas I was more of an OK-to-do type. They just didn't seem to have any taste. For a moment I thought I might have found more kindred spirits if I'd taken on an Architecture course, but I also knew I'd never have the discipline to complete such a complex degree. I decided to ignore my classmates as much as possible, except the few I had some connection with.

I started to come alive and really express myself as the course progressed. There were subjects I didn't like or just didn't get, but mostly I was happy, and liking what I was doing. The faculty was only a couple of blocks away from my grandmother Helena's house, and I used to often stop over for lunch and a visit. I could tell my grandparents were getting older and a bit more inward looking. My grandfather Armando more so. He was always happy to see me, and after the initial greeting he would return to his rocking chair in the dark hall, which moved gently as the old clock announced the tyranny of time passing. I close my eyes and see him there, as if it was today. Imagine if thoughts are an electrical impulse that connects to an event that is still happening in quantum time, time eternal? I wonder what my grandad was thinking about, maybe a jump into his own time travel event, to a time when he was young and full of life. But those were not my concerns back then.

The art college was whispering a new idea into my mind, after I had been experimenting with photography, which was taking almost all of my time and energy. We could borrow professional cameras and lenses and go out photographing people and places around the college, for specific projects. But what I liked most was taking my rolls of film to the dark room afterwards and spend a whole morning developing them and copying negatives onto paper. I loved the glow of the red lamp and the cavernous smell of the concrete walls, the white trays full of chemicals, the giant plastic tweezers hanging from lines like clumsy acrobats, the drip dripping of water on the steel sheets, the imposing shadow of a row of enlargers, the silent revelation of secrets I only half knew. Who needed boyfriends when all this was available just for me? I'd forgotten all about those exotic creatures and didn't seem in a hurry to find me one. I was too excited at the prospect of someday making moving pictures, because photography had inspired me to think I could make films someday.

I had left music behind for a while after my return from England, but it didn't last long. My friend Rita the bassist was playing in João's new band, which was called *Toshiro and the Dumb Girls*. Toshiro was a friend of his, a genius astronomer and one of the only people in Brazil who could play stick bass. Me and Rita were the actual 'dumb girls' for having refused to join his band, although Rita eventually did, but the name stuck, nevertheless. *The Dumb Girls* didn't play or rehearse often enough, it was more of an odd project. Rita had met a couple who were starting a new band, and somehow, she convinced them that I was the missing link. She set up a meeting between us, we all got on well and the next step was to set up a rehearsal to see how we got on musically. But I felt affinity with them and assumed we'd naturally be able to work together. Nuno was the singer & guitarist, Vera his wife and second guitarist. They had a small studio in their basement and that was where we first tried some tunes together. I guessed it would work, and it did. And thus, the next 3 years of my life with Compartment started, which I did not guess would be so full of energy, drama, jealousy and discovery.

I felt even more appreciated and listened to as an artist this time, perhaps because there were 3 girls and one guy. No big egos except for

Nuno, but we took it with a lightness of heart and humour. He had started *Cyclops*, another band which had hit the big time after he left, and it seemed he was in search of absolute commitment to artistic purity. I was too young to know better, but to a certain extent this inspired me. We spent roughly a year writing and rehearsing enough material for gigs and an album and started to do the São José nightclubs round. I could fit my entire drumkit in my dad's old banger, plus Rita's amp and bass. There were good venues, there were bad venues, but all were a chance for us to sharpen our skills. I don't recall being paid a cent during that time, or maybe only peanuts. And all the while I was balancing the band with my art college activities. I had also been offered to attend my aunt's printing course at her USJ Architecture foundation course, and was having great fun experimenting with linos, wood printing and all sorts of 'new' media.

On those days I really felt as if the world was my oyster. I was expressing all this stuff I never knew I had inside of me. Our relationship as a band became deeper, as we rehearsed at least 3 times a week, socialised, saw Cure and Cocteau Twins gigs, ate and talked together. We did a couple of road trips outside the city to look for photo locations, one of which was down south to the port of Santos, made infamous by the English explorer Richard Burton during his time there as Consul in the 1800s: he described it as a diseased scorching swamp, with 'ants as big as bats'. It was definitely hot and humid, but Burton was a friend of hyperbole. We took the old imperial highway which snaked down the mountain, offering majestic views of the sea beyond, with old road markers covered in Portuguese tiles. I think we drove down in Nuno and Vera's battered old VW Beetle, but it served to bond us further into some dysfunctional wedlock.

After a long period of practice and gigs, with our cult reputation flourishing, we got the news that *PMT*, a big pop band in Brazil, was starting a music label and we were to be their first hire. They got us a professional studio, with 23 channels – 23! To us that was beyond luxurious. I had my own drum annexe. We had pop star visits at the studio and 2 special participations in the album. It was hard but rewarding work. Our producer was PMT's manager Lauro. He was a settling and protective presence for us, and had great knowledge of music and keyboards especially, but by God I hated his taste in drum sounds. I really didn't know how to assert myself or even voice my objection to something. I couldn't even assert myself to MYSELF – I knew I had a real problem with the snare drum sound Lauro had just chosen, but I told myself he knew more than me and so I should delegate. I haven't listened to our record in decades, but somehow, I can still hear that raspy metallic sound without any of the richness I thought the songs deserved. Over all I thought some of the songs had a bit too much of a manicured triumphant spirit to them, but there's no way I would have been able to express this thought back then. It would have existed as a discomfort but not as words.

But despite my reservations about some of the flourishes our producer added to the record, it was a work of love and it showed. I was proud of what we had achieved. Next item on the agenda was album design cover, which I naturally thought would be my job, but Nuno had other plans. His friend, famous designer Fatimah Santos was a fan and wanted to do it as a gift, so the job went to her. I didn't mind it so much in the end because I liked what she did; I thought it was classy and a good synthesis of our sound. The album was called *Eastbourne Blues*. It came from my time in Eastbourne, where, while sat in a café holding a mug of hot tea, I heard a bossa nova track drifting through the cold February afternoon. That moment seemed to be the confluence of ideas, and I suggested this to the band as a title for an album. They agreed, and it incited many questions from the press in the days and months that followed. Curiously, Nuno developed the habit of claiming the idea for the album title as his own, and I disputed it a few times until I gave up. It was enough that I and the others knew it had been my idea, and it was just ONE idea anyway. But the gift of hindsight is a miracle indeed. I had never had such a complex relationship, or any relationship for that matter, with an ego driven narcissist, albeit a tame one. It was clear that Nuno had a constant need for attention, and he was in the perfect position to get it from 3 awestruck females. He was very talented, as a lyricist and a musician. I wasn't entirely convinced by his voice, but it was part of the entire package.

The recording of our album went on for about a month, more or less. We'd had a meeting with a lawyer, to determine financial arrangements, but I was oblivious to what any of it meant. There were small money advances being made to Nuno and Vera, less so to Rita. I foolishly gave up on any money owed to me for the time being so that the others, especially the couple, who had a home and a small daughter to support, could survive. I reasoned that I was being supported by my father and I could perfectly well hold on until the formal payment came through. This proved to be a big mistake because I never saw any money from the sale of any records. Not one cent. I wasn't a big hit, but it must have sold a few thousand copies. Maybe that was the way of record labels, I just didn't know. But the PMT label folded right after the release of our album, which still had mostly positive reviews. We did manage to go to Rio on an all-expenses-paid trip, staying at the Copacabana Palace and hanging out with the big popstars of the day. There was a lot of cocaine going around those days, but I wasn't a big fan. I didn't even like drink much.

There was one party we went to – as a band, which was almost like going as a couple – hosted by one of the members of Cyclops. It was a big house with a garden, and I ended up snorting cocaine for the first time, probably goaded on by the others. It's like this: if you are having a creative relationship with someone, you need to at least travel the same wavelength for a bit or know what if feels like. Nobody said this to me, but I sensed it as some unspoken rule. I figured it wouldn't hurt to try. I think I just had one or two lines of the stuff, and it took about 30 mins to have any impact on me. I hated it. First it threw me into a big depressive hole, and next I found myself talking non-stop to people I didn't know about private issues close to my heart. It was like a disaster film unfolding from the outside of me. I promised myself I'd never touch cocaine again. Even the smell of it made me sick. I wasn't very keen on hash or marijuana either, but these were easier to manage, and I did smoke it a few times. But I never did out of my own will, it was always an obligation that I thought was expected of me, in order to join in. Not that it wasn't fun sometimes. But after-effects like hunger for the trashiest food possible and the feeling I'd slept for a whole week taught me to stand up for myself and just refuse to smoke it if I didn't feel like it. I always found it a bit alarming to see how many people use marijuana. Certainly, most of the people I knew, perhaps not so much now because my closest friends are on a similar path to me and that excludes any drugs and drink most times. I always felt it was a pollution of my inner environment but wasn't assertive enough to say it out loud. Maybe I thought people would think me judgemental, and in all honesty, I was, and still am, sometimes, but age has given me the option of flicking the switch to 'I don't care what you think'.

Things got complicated suddenly and quickly for the band when Nuno and I started an affair, at the same time we set off to translate Jim Morrison's poetry book The Lords and The New Creatures. I never saw it coming, the development of my deep admiration for his erudition being transmuted into romance. It seems I was the only one. Even his wife Vera could smell it coming, and I think he'd also had a prospective fling with Rita. Everyone just accepted that was the way he was. It wasn't a very happy time for me because it pretty much imploded the band. I was an ingenue who'd still never had much experience of men or dating, and suddenly I'd thrown myself into this vortex of emotions and conflicting intentions. A subtle tug of war started between me and Vera, each taking turns in claiming Nuno's intimacy and affections, but not all of it worked in synch, which caused a lot of hurt and anger. Rita was stuck in the middle and not very happy about it. No one was happy about any of it, except for Nuno, who relished the attention from two women. I'm not sure how we didn't have a massive falling out sooner, or how we managed to continue being a band with all this shit going down.

But eventually the wheels did fall off. Vera had confronted me a couple of times, in a pretty civilized way, but I didn't know what to say. I was perplexed by it. How can this woman, whose husband I've more or less stolen, speak to me as a friend? Perhaps because we were friends…I relied on my total lack of experience and shyness to serve as an excuse for my actions. I really did believe people should cut me some major slack because I felt a bit like a child sometimes, even at 23 years old. The band continued to practice and plan gigs, we even went to a TV show hosted by a friend, but our engine had been busted. No one declared the band extinct. It became so; just like wildlife. Resentment brewed from all sides. There were some final harsh words exchanged between me and Vera. I met Nuno at, of all places, a leafy square near his house, because I wouldn't go there anymore. He seemed distant and sobered by the whole sad affair and said I should go clean things up with his wife! I said I'd already told her what I thought she wanted to hear. It turns out this last phrase caused a misunderstanding because days later I got a call from Rita asking to see me for a chat. When we met, she pretty much relayed to me how all three of them thought my statement had been hypocritical, as if I'd told Vera some fake words just to get her off my back. As I explained to Rita what

I'd actually meant (that Vera wanted the truth and I complied), I started to wonder why I was bothering to justify myself on any level to these people, who appeared to have put me on trial. I thought they knew me better than that. I thought I knew them better than that. It was a moment of reckoning and growth, when I first learned how to stand up for myself. I didn't do anything outrageous or pyrotechnic, although there was a bonfire of vanities of some sort; I said goodbye to the three of them and decided to go lick my wounds in Miami and Richmond, US.

Unlike my English adventures, I hadn't planned this trip. I didn't even think of going to England again, which speaks volumes about my frame of mind. My mother could see how upset and downtrodden I was by the whole Compartment episode and thought I could benefit by going away for a while. She suggested I stay with her friend Madalena for a month or so and I agreed. The change of scenery and lack of anyone too close to me would be beneficial. Madalena's house was in West Boca Raton, a nice and quiet beach suburb well to the north of Miami. I didn't know what a time of contemplation meant but that was precisely what I experienced. Madalena and her husband Demis were quiet and worked from home, and I could explore the neighbourhood by foot, or by car whenever I could borrow their old Mitsubishi. They lived in an old 1930s Spanish colonial style house with a small garden at the back, where orange trees mixed with foliage long forgotten. I'd go outside to get oranges every morning for a fresh juice and that is what I mostly remember as the thing that cleared my mind and brightened my day, every day. I froze out having ever played with Compartment for at least a whole month, helped in great part by the absence of the internet, Facebook, WhatsApp or emails back in the late 1980s. Madalena suggested I go visit her daughter Atlanta who was doing an Arts degree up in Richmond. I could get a train there and it would take about 5 hours, but the trip was scenic, and I could also see a bit of the deep south on the way to Virginia.

I remember being at the platform and just about to board the train when I noticed a tall, handsome blonde guy giving me the eye. I guess I was learning flirting on the hoof because I held his gaze for just the right amount of time before we all boarded. I found my seat was next to an elderly black lady who seemed very friendly, except I couldn't understand a word she said. I think she had a sort of hood slang which my knowledge of English couldn't reach, but we got on well, sharing snacks and the like. I decided to go and get a drink at the bar carriage. As I waited for my turn I realized tall blonde guy was there, eyeballing me again. I went back to my seat, but I could sniff an incoming adventure. Minutes later the same guy walks past my seat and on to the next few carriages and returns back to the bar carriage, sending me a loaded look as he walks past my seat again. Talk about boarding a train to the unknown! Ingenue turned vixen in a few weeks.

I went back to the bar, bought another drink and sat at a table near the window. Minutes later he appears, asking if he can join me. We started with some polite conversation, which then went on to the ring I was wearing and how that ring was perched on a lovely finger, which was attached to a lovely hand, and soon enough I was following this guy to his private compartment. It happened so fast I didn't even have time to think, but I suspect I would have done the same regardless. I remember moving upwards with the landscape rushing past me on his window. Bearing in mind I was actually still pretty naïve, so oral sex meant nothing to me, and I probably literally sat on his face as the world spun outside. He fell asleep straight away (or maybe passed out after my vaginal muzzle) and I was restless, didn't know what to do. I decided to get dressed and leave, buzzing with adrenaline but also embarrassment.

I wondered if anyone in that train had followed what happened, but no one took any notice of me as I glided back to my seat. The old black lady was asleep by now, having put on hair rollers and a hair net on while I was gone. As the train stops came and went, some more seats became vacant, and I moved carriages just in case my one-train-stand came looking for me. I knew he was getting off in South Carolina because he'd mentioned it - before the conversation got more intentional. When the train alighted at his station, I watched the platform from behind a curtain, and saw him there looking at windows, perhaps trying to spot me. I didn't want him to see me. I asked myself how I could have been so reckless, but I think I was secretly trying to implode my past behaviours in the sex and romance department. It wasn't that I was ashamed of being thought of as a slut or similar (well maybe a bit), but it was more about wanting to shift my own concept of who I was. So, I made peace with myself and realized nothing was lost, except I'd left one of my earrings in his compartment. I reckoned that was a symbolic loss of another virginity.

I had a great time with Atlanta, who shared an apartment in a bohemian area of Richmond with an on/off boyfriend called Desmond. I think I only spent a few days with her, but they were full of new ideas, people and places. She was at Art college like me and seemed especially interested in Photography. We went around this beautiful city taking shots of each other, going to bars, cafes and even an Ethiopian restaurant, where the food was pots of different stews served with a flabby flat bread, which doesn't sound great, but it was actually delicious. I'd always been a big fan of Edgar Allan Poe and to my surprise there was a statue of him at the University of Richmond. Atlanta took photos of me pretending to talk to his statue or kneeling by him, as if I was worshipping him. This would have been a time when his writings were foremost in my mind, so when Atlanta suggested we go visit his gravesite I didn't think twice. We had a bit of an adventure there, because on arrival we realised the gates to the cemetery had just been shut. Atlanta said, 'let's climb the wall' and I hesitated for a moment, which lasted only until I became aware this was a unique opportunity, never to be repeated. I was carrying some plastic red roses and laid them at the foot of his mausoleum, while Atlanta clicked some more shots. It was almost sunset and a perfect Poe moment.

Atlanta's on/off boyfriend Desmond was friendly enough, and it wasn't entirely clear what kind of relationship they had. He picked me up at the train station while Atlanta was at college the day I arrived. She let me have her bedroom and moved to Desmond's room during my stay. I'd never heard of an on/off relationship and they seemed detached enough from each other. We were all chatting one day, and I must have said something about my physical low self-esteem because she turned to him and said I was beautiful, and didn't he agree? He said, 'that's how I could tell it was her at the station'. I was flattered even if I thought it was an odd thing to say next to your girlfriend. He was a bit odd, sometimes poking his head in the room I was in without knocking. The fact that there was no door, only a curtain, didn't help matters much. And when the three of us were out having drinks once, he suddenly suggested a 3-way kiss on the lips, to which we complied but to me it just confirmed there was something a bit out of kilter going on. Months or years later I heard from Madalena that Desmond was a bit obsessive and Atlanta had got a restraining order against him after she'd moved home and heart. But back to those sweet March days in Virginia it didn't seem that way. I once nearly walked in on them having sex. To go from my room to Desmond's room I needed to cross kitchen and bathroom, and as I got to the kitchen I started to hear oohms and moans, and I called out for Atlanta. No reply, just some more similar noises, and I kept moving towards their room but something about those noises told me to stop. I'd never heard the sounds of orgasm or climax, or knew what it felt like, but my instinct told me these sounds were sex related. Back in my room I felt a strange sense of wonder, as if I'd just got a glimpse of a fabulous unknown world.

My time in the US flew by like it was a dream. I was back in São José and back to the band conundrum. Rita got in touch with me to say that Nuno had been angry at my leaving the country with no warning or explanation. I couldn't believe his sense of entitlement and wondered what planet those people lived in. I decided to just let it be and never returned his calls. I declared that chapter of my life a case closed and decided to forget music for a while. My sister had recently got a job as bartender/manager at an Irish pub in a hip and well-to-do area of São José, and soon she offered me some work waiting tables and serving behind the bar. Foyle's pub was owned by three larger than life lotharios, all of them bon-vivants, drinkers and entertainers. Dutchman Bart lived at an annex in the attic, looked like a portrait Frans Hals might have painted on a bad day and was the most relaxed and interesting of them, living vicariously through his business. The other two, Irish Paddy and Heinz, a Swiss Brazilian lover of whisky, were constantly on site, smooching customers and chatting up the female waiting staff. I didn't mind that so much because they weren't creepy. And men would be men, that was the way of the land, especially in a country like Brazil. I probably only worked at Foyle's for about a year, but it was great fun, I immersed myself further in being connected to people my own age, which sometimes ended up in late night drinking sessions at the ancient 1940s Riviera bar. But since I'd spent my whole young life not really doing any of that I thought it was a good time to at least see what the fuss was about. I found it more fun than expected, even if I did notice an underbelly of recurring people whose eyes seemed to have no light within. Suspended in a halo of youth and lives just beginning, all the girls behind the bar and waiting tables became a team, and for a while it felt like I was on top of the world. Around this time, we also managed to get backstage passes to a couple of big gigs. I don't think I'll ever forget the sight of James Brown coming to say hello to us after his concert, dressed in a white fur coat and giant orange shades, his trademark bouffant hair glinting with sweat and hair gel. His manager fancied one of my friends, whose looks got us into most of the backstage VIP rooms of the late 80s, which were also awash with drugs. Cocaine was a big thing in São José, but I decided drugs were definitely not my thing. Drinks, mostly spirits I actually enjoyed, especially cognac or rum in cocktails. At Foyle's, we got wages plus our choice of a meal from the menu per shift, which was either fried beef or chicken and French fries, plus all the booze we could manage. The kitchen boys were constantly making us more food during our shifts. I got to know tons of people, most of them foreigners who seemed to be lured by 'the only legit pub in town'. It was also where I met my new band mates, led by a guitarist called Peri.

His full name was Peri Vanucci, a confluence of his parents' Italian roots and taste for Native Brazilian folk tales. He was sat having beers with other musicians at Foyle's one night and he recognized me from Compartment. I thought that was a first. I wondered what I'd do if he asked me for an autograph – the only one I'd signed so far was for our one committed fan who'd seen all our gigs. But he asked me to join his new band instead. I was curious, and if I'm honest I quite fancied him as well, unconcerned by the recent erosion of my last band due to misplaced romantic affections. But him and his band were often there, and I ended up attending one of their rehearsals. It was a bit testosterone heavy, but then I'd only been in bands with a high female demographic and I could feel the difference in balance. I decided to join the band anyway, because I missed having that sort of camaraderie. I didn't actually love the music, or the band's name, *Odore di Figa*. It meant 'smell of __*expletive for female genitalia_*' in Italian and thinking it funny the band told me I now justified their name. It was a mish mash of styles, with a sort of hard rock aesthetic but a more bluesy sound. There was an Argentinian guitarist with a black mop of hair. The bassist was tall and blonde, with a red bandana, and owned a record shop called Kristallnacht. I didn't know what that meant, although I'm almost certain that he did. But he wasn't a Nazi, it was probably more to do with a punk spirit of shock and awe, like calling a band Joy Division. The last guy was Rocco the singer, although I don't remember him ever doing that. He was a bit full of himself because he had classic Roman features and a girlfriend who seemed permanently attached to him.

So, I joined this rag tag band of characters more out of longing than genuine inclination. And my crush on Peri only increased. I thought it was a well-kept secret that only I and perhaps he knew. He looked like a cross between The Cure's Robert Smith and John Lennon but dressed like a toned-down version of the Sisters of Mercy. A long black mullet completed the look and I thought he was dreamy. I sensed he might reciprocate my feelings, but no words or actions came my way, so I decided to write him a letter to tell him how I felt. I was a bit more daring those days, but not much, and I knew I could spell out my feelings so much better with written words. I don't remember where we met after he'd read it, but essentially, he told me he saw me as a friend only. I was disappointed but not distraught. Somehow, I sensed he'd chickened out of even considering dating me, but I wasn't convinced of his indifference. Eventually I lost interest in the band and I didn't even have to jump out because everyone else had decided it wasn't worth it. I saw less of Peri, but absence did not make the heart grow fonder.

I dated a couple of other people I met at Foyle's, but they were only snogs stolen in weird circumstances. I also dated my sister's British boss for a couple of weeks, he was the head of an indie recording label which brought acts like Cocteau Twins to Brazil. His name was Stewart and he was into the porn underbelly of São José. It only took a few dates for me to realize I was way out of my depth with this guy. He was actually a nice man, with very dysfunctional sexual habits and probably loved playing the wealthy gringo card with the high-class whores we sometimes met at dodgy clubs late at night. I was getting a bit dysfunctional myself. One night, I think it was at some crazy New Year's Eve party in an old derelict club that I bumped into Peri again, whilst out with Stewart. Peri was suddenly all over me, wooing me and leading me outside for a private 'chat', only a few months after publicly but kindly rejecting me. Stewart had disappeared with a couple of women and was nowhere to be found. Outside, Peri kissed me, but I didn't see stars anywhere, like I imagined I would. He said he did, although it seemed an exaggeration. I wasn't on his wavelength and felt sorry that our timing was all wrong, but there it was. That was one of the rare moments in my youth when I felt I could handle this whole romance business with a sense of humour. It didn't last long.

Rita had been in touch with me on and off during my time in band wilderness. She couldn't understand why I was wasting my time with Peri and his friends, and of course she was right. Maybe I also had the need to assert myself in terms of being able to find my own opportunities, but she had a new and interesting offer nevertheless, for an all-female band. It would be the two of us, plus Moara, a girl she'd met recently and got on with straight away. I generally trusted Rita's instinct and was a bit fed up with being in mixed bands, because there was always some trouble or sexual tension brewing, so I agreed. She took me to meet Moara at her mum's place, a 1950s house in the most desirable, old-money part of São José. Her house was great, a bit messy, but surrounded by beautiful mango trees which threw geometric shades over the garden. Her mum was an aspiring filmmaker, and it was probably the first time I'd met someone who actually made films, even if they were short experimental ones. Moara lived alone with her mum, sometimes visited by her artist brother who at that time was part of a sort of artists' co-op called Tenda 8, along with Rita's boyfriend and 5 other guys. They only seemed to hang out with each other and their girlfriends, finish each other's sentences and laugh at each other's jokes. I wasn't very inspired by art as a collective endeavour, especially such an incestuous one. Art collectives such as the Secessionists or the Pre-Raphaelite brotherhood had produced some amazing ground-breaking work, but I wasn't so sure some of the Tenda 8 guys weren't moved by ego more than soul.

But what about us making music? I loved it but always felt there was something beyond music calling me before I could reach out for it. Sometimes I would find myself wondering if there wasn't more to life than this constant yearning for the next thing. I'd started my seeking for something to add meaning to life round about the time I began listening to classical music, or any music that touched my heart. Edgar Allan Poe's stories and tales, Maxfield Parish paintings, the writings of Nietzsche and Schopenhauer, and films. When I was a young child, I'd spend hours looking at a historical encyclopaedia with various biographies of famous people like Napoleon, Da Vinci, Joan of Arc, Van Gogh, full of famous paintings to illustrate them. I'd say that was my introduction to what lies beyond art. Those pictures moved me, at the age of 6 or 7, when I didn't even know what being moved meant. Playing music now at 25 or so, I was struck by how similar this sense of wonder was. There's always an ego-soul equation involved in the production of art, but with an artists' collective I could see how that could get complicated very quickly.

With the new band things seemed to fall into place with ease, which had actually happened with 400B and Compartment, but this time there were no men to distract us. We still needed to find a fourth member, a singer and sometimes guitar player, and this happened very quickly. Our old 400B friend João was recording a tribute album to one of the original members of a psychedelic 60s band. He was producer and curator, and sometimes singer. He asked the three of us to do backing vocals on one of the tracks, and there we were joined by Charlotte, a Belgian girl who was going out with Toshiro. The moment I heard her singing I thought I was hearing an angel. It was obvious to me she should join our band. Rita took no convincing, Moara a bit more, because she thought it would be odd to have someone singing with an accent. I thought that was a ludicrous reason why she shouldn't join us, and with strength in numbers Charlotte came to our first rehearsal. I'd convinced my grandmother to let us use one of the rooms in her basement, which was like a ghost sitting room, perfectly decked for a post dinner party chat, except it was always shut. We all loved our sessions there, me because it was a chance to see my grandparents 3 times a week, and the others because there was always coffee and freshly made cakes after rehearsals. My grandmother also loved the opportunity to talk to younger people. She sometimes felt a bit locked in a mausoleum because my grandad was perfectly happy to sit in the dark hall and listen to the big clock echoing time in his mind's eye. I'm pretty sure he didn't think much of our music, but he always liked to see me.

Out of all the people I played with I thought this lot was the best. I suggested we call the band Illumination, based on some of Jim Morrison's poetry describing the first place where the moving image was exhibited as a spectacle to paying customers. The girls loved it and so we set out to build a repertoire, make some demos and conquer the world. Truth be told, as I finished my arts degree and dove deeper into the world of film I wondered if music was 100% my calling. I'd been using all my free time going to the cinema, on my own, just to appease my hungry eyes. There was one week during half term when I watched a film every single day, and nearly all of those remain in my list of favourites. One of them was Dead Poets Society, which absolutely floored me and to this day still does, whenever I review it. Another favourite was Wings of Desire, which I haven't seen since, but the impact of it lives at the back of my brain somewhere. The thing about films was that it wasn't just images, but it was images with music and writing, which were the three things I most loved immersing myself in. But the ambition of making films was far too distant in my own desire for the time being.

We never managed to take the band forward, even if we did write a few perfect pop songs, played gigs which became legendary, recorded a couple of demo tapes and got on perfectly with each other. We were support act for a couple of big Brazilian bands, got our own band stylist, and had articles written for pop journals and magazines announcing us as the next big thing. In all this I had a mixture of excitement and consternation. I wasn't sure I wanted to be styled, but I tried it on. I wasn't alone in feeling a bit ridiculously overdressed, like a toy soldier. I could tell the others were also a bit reticent about it, but we played the gig anyhow. We played other cities, again opening for a big band in a wine festival. I'd never seen such a huge audience, I felt as if we were in some sort of Live Aid, which looked overwhelming from the stage. I think the winds of musical change started to blow, and suddenly we weren't seeing 100% eye to eye anymore. It was like we were moving to our difficult second album, without having ever released the first one.

But the thing that derailed the band's future, which probably worked in my favour, was Charlotte's return to Belgium. I think she never meant to stay in São José forever, it was just the end of an adventure. Like any Northern European person, she wanted to cycle everywhere but the city wasn't built for cyclists, so it was either risking death or injury or pollution in the lungs on a daily basis. She and Toshiro decided to move to Brussels for good, which set my mind on thinking I could do the same. Not move to Belgium but expand my horizons elsewhere. After Charlotte was gone, we tried to get other people to join, but our band was alchemically perfect and without an original member it could fall apart, which it did. We did play a few more gigs trying out various people joining us, friends from other bands and Moara's boyfriend, a singer with a good voice but zero style awareness. He had a poodle perm, round glasses and a taste for 1970s Brazilian folk music. In other words, Charlotte's departure was the perfect coda.

So here I was, 3 bands later having earned no money, at the end of my arts degree, not a dazzling backlog in the area of relationships, and as usual I didn't know what to do. I started to write some articles for a movie magazine some of my musician/ journalists edited, mostly on the subject of horror films. That was actually fun, being sent to dark booths to watch Troma movies and write about them. I learned a lot about cheap horror exploitation filmmaking, theoretically at least. Troma had titles like *Surf Nazis Must Die* and *Redneck Zombies,* and I found myself watching this stuff and wondering what its aim was, apart from shock and horror. I much preferred the Re-Animator series, which were still ludicrous and amateurish but at least it was based on HP Lovecraft stories, which I'd recently discovered, and there was a palpable passion behind what they did. They were like a second-rate version of the Roger Corman films, which were also cheaply made, but these guys made Corman films look big budget by comparison.

I wrote the articles, but I still felt clueless. I didn't know anything about film, only that I was passionate about it. I also started to work as a translator, tagging Portuguese subtitles onto English language films. My aunt got me the job, and I tried it on for a couple of films. My first job was on Dr Zhivago, which was a three-hour film full of dialogue, whereas the guy on the booth next to me had The Emerald Forest, which must have had one page of dialogue for the entire film. I don't think I lasted beyond the David Lean classic, because I found the job deeply depressing. It was almost like watching from the outside of a house where a magical party was happening, and not being able to go inside. Maybe it was a blessing in disguise, whereby looking at this artistry, this wonderful craft, made me realise I wanted to go in and join the party.

Meanwhile, my sister had left our parents' house, much to their consternation. She'd started bringing some 'challenging' friends back home, and also a couple of boyfriends to spend the night which didn't go down very well with my father. I think she had been planning to leave but that was the push she needed. She rented a small apartment about 15-minute drive from us and got a job as a receptionist at serviced flats nearby. I was surprised by her choice of work, but she could be very appealing and gregarious when she chose to be, and soon enough she became the shining star at reception. I knew it wasn't exactly what she wanted, but it would do until she decided her own future. And because she hadn't finished school, it was harder to find better paid jobs, but she could at least have fun and meet lots of different people. The Foyle's days were gone, and I think we'd all got bored with late night drinking sessions with the same people. We had been collectively mugged one night, outside the local café, where a gang of skinheads clashed with a couple of punk boys we knew. Caught in the crossfire, I was hit in the mouth by something metallic and passed out. I regained consciousness to find my sister gently slapping my face as I lay on the pavement. My handbag was missing, and so was my weekly pay check. We had to return home and relate to my mum what had happened, as if my swollen mouth hadn't already told half the tale. I wasn't too bothered about my poor lips, but the loss of my hard-earned cash was deeply felt. The result of a week of long shifts and standing up for hours, gone. For a while there was a fire of pure hatred burning in me, which completely took me by surprise. I would have advocated the death penalty for the guy who nicked my handbag. Such is human nature, from pacifist to extremist in the blink of an eye.

At the corporate flats, my sister met an English couple who remained friends with her after they moved to their new home. She used to babysit for them when they had a rare date night, and she once got me to replace her as babysitter. I was quite happy to chat to them and look after their baby son for no pay, given my yearning for a connection to anything British, or anyone who reminded me of it. I babysat for them a few times, but they insisted on paying me which at first, I resisted. Eventually I realised it was a bit odd of me to refuse money and why would I do that? My employment record hadn't been brilliant so far and so I gladly took the cash. The husband, a Northerner called Keith, drove me back home once, being very chatty and unusually friendly. I started to tell him about my assault and my swollen lips. We were at traffic lights and he touched my mouth, as if to say, 'oh no poor you'. But I felt a frisson of I don't know what. Could he be making a pass at me? When he dropped me off he suddenly snogged me as I was about to leave. I could taste whisky in his mouth. He held me close and said he wanted to make love to me. I was completely shocked, not expecting that at all, which is not to say I didn't like it. I went home, he drove off, each left to their own thoughts. I think he called me a couple of days later, because I think I used that old subterfuge, my favourite way of expressing feelings: I wrote him a letter. I found out from my sister where he worked but had to tell her why I wanted his address. She was a bit surprised to hear of Keith's indiscretion, but advised me not to expect much. I expected nothing and everything, that's how confused I was. Eventually he called me and apologised, saying he'd had a bit to drink and maybe it was the settled married life that spurred him to consider straying. He was honest and direct, and I had no reason to doubt his sincerity. I wasn't in any rush to get involved with another married man and this put an end to anything I might have regretted later. But it wasn't the last time I would fool around with a married man.

My sister had started corresponding with an New Zealander who was based in Belgium, and this being 1990, they communicated mostly by post. As their connection felt stronger, they were faxing each other nearly every day, until eventually he invited her over for Christmas in New Zealand. My mother was suspicious and quite concerned about whether my sister wouldn't get herself involved in some criminal enterprise, or worse, become a victim of sex traffic. We didn't know anything about this chap Bernard, but my sister decided to go anyway. As soon as she got there she called us and made sure we knew our fears were unfounded. He seemed to be a good guy and they were having a great time. It sounded like she didn't want to come back to Brazil and that New Zealand was the best place she'd ever known. After about a month she did come back but her head was somewhere else, and she couldn't wait to be reunited with Bernard. Eventually they settled in Brussels, where he was working as a computer programmer and apparently earning lots of money. They married in Auckland, she returned for about a month and just like that, POOF she was gone.

I had also started to correspond with a Scottish man who lived in London. Back in the 1990s there would be ads placed in papers like Loot or its Brazilian equivalent, a lonely hearts-type column, except no one would admit they'd be searching for their soulmate, it came across more in a spirit of camaraderie. I'd had pen pals before when I was a kid, either from some magazine club or foreign comics we used to get from abroad. I loved it when letters arrived and could tell from the envelopes who it was, even before I spotted the handwriting. I never met those people, they were usually from somewhere else in Brazil or abroad, but that wasn't the point. It was the build-up of a relationship which everyone involved knew would never materialize, but it was fun anyway. With my Scottish correspondent that wasn't the case. We exchanged a few letters, and I needed a break because of my grandfather Armando's death, which happened in a short space of time.

He wasn't ill. My parents had gone to Portugal on a short holiday with my aunt and uncle, and he had some sort of health issue in the meantime. Later we realised he must have had a mild stroke, but at first sight I think he had the wrong diagnosis and that worsened his condition because it brought on more stress. The day my parents arrived I picked them up and tried not to alarm my mother, but we all went straight to the hospital he'd been admitted to. I think he got moved from there on to another one, and then home, but he deteriorated quickly. I heard him dissing my grandmother one day, in a way he normally wouldn't unless he wasn't quite himself. On the few days before he died there was a flurry of confusion in his house. I'd sit with my grandmother holding her hand, having never seen her looking so vulnerable. I saw him one last time lying on his bed, but he didn't look like the grandfather I knew. There was a translucent quality to his whole physical appearance, and I felt he wasn't long for this world. He was the first person I was close to whose death I felt deeply. I didn't go to the funeral, but I don't remember why. I guess I wanted to remember him as the quirky special grandad he was, not as a body in a casket under the earth.

But life carried on as it usually does, and I was back to my correspondence. My pen pal's name was Bill, and he seemed keen on coming to visit me. I was a bit surprised by the speed at which this was going, if it was indeed what I thought it might be; we had been getting a bit flirty in our letters and I suddenly panicked slightly at the prospect of seeing him standing outside my doorway. I had managed to move into my mother's office, which was a block away. It was a small 2-bedroom apartment, but perfect for the sense of independence I needed. I still

117

wasn't earning anything, but wrote articles on film here and there, and was starting to try my hand at writing screenplays. I couldn't afford to pay rent. The arrangement was that I wasn't allowed to change anything much but could treat the apartment as my home. I had a house warming party one night which lasted until 4 am and caused the management to harass me and threaten to call the police if we didn't keep the music down, my first taste of being responsible for a living space. This happened during a period in which I'd finished college, Illumination had slowly faded away and I had no paid employment. I could see no opportunities anywhere and at this moment in my life, Bill announced he'd bought a ticket to Brazil.

I was anxious and excited to finally meet him. He'd sent pictures, presumably the most flattering ones he had. I'd done the same. So, all that was left was for us to meet in real life. I picked him up at the airport and drove him home, thinking that he looked a bit bulkier in real life - but still quite alluring. I don't know what he was thinking but he was quite a talker. I don't know if we got together straight away but I think it took a couple of days and it happened quite naturally. Suddenly we were in my bed having sex, and still at this point I didn't really have much of a clue, but I recall it as a good experience. In fact, it was probably the first time I experienced an orgasm, or at least what I thought an orgasm felt like. It was very different and very pleasurable. I had no idea if I'd caused it or he had, but I ran with it. This was before condoms and STDs awareness had become widespread and I don't remember us having used protection, but maybe there was an angel at my side making sure nothing happened. I introduced Bill to my parents, took him to our beach house in the Atlantic rain forest and also to Rio de Janeiro. And then he was gone, back to London.

I had been planning to return to England again and this was the excuse I needed. I'd told Bill I was thinking of visiting him and trying to get a place for a postgrad or a film course at Central Saint Martins, a prestigious film & art school in London. But first I had to convince my father this was the best solution for my current unemployment. There really seemed to be no opportunities for film work in Brazil in the early 1990s. The only possibility was to go back to university and study film, but that would have meant another 4 years of my life and perhaps a future job as a film lecturer or academic, an option that filled me with dread. It was also around this time or even earlier that I can trace the start of my search for spirituality and meaning to my life, although if asked then I probably would not have described it as such. I was interested in radiesthesia, dowsing, numerology and tarot readings, and trying to map my life in terms of what the gods might have in store. It never occurred to me that I may actually have some say and some power in how my life evolved. Instead I had a deep faith in destiny, and fate - its grumpier sibling.

I think my father thought I was going a bit doolally. He'd arrive at the apartment and find all my copper plates with crystals and bits of paper with the destination 'London' underneath them. He actually voiced such concerns to me, and I didn't know what to say. We'd had a heart to heart in which he confessed he was worried about my future and what I planned to do with my life, because I didn't seem to be giving him and my mother many pointers until now. I must have seemed really desperate for meaning and direction, because I remember I started to cry and beg him to pay for my trip to London and that I seemed to have no future where I was. Thinking back to those days, the sense that there was something inexorably driving me to leave was palpable. Whatever I said to him worked; I made it to England at around the end of March 1992, to stay with Bill for a month and see what short film courses I could find – but also to find out where I was at with my life.

ON STARTING LIFE
IN ENGLAND

Before I left for England I had exchanged quite a few letters with Bill, in anticipation of us meeting again. One of those letters was written when I was feeling at my highest expression of love, and I poured it all over him with words. The response was not what I expected. It was more of a muted letter. I was puzzled and a bit ashamed for wearing my heart on my sleeve so childishly, I thought. But with the excitement of the trip I forgot about the letter or my fear of what he might have made of it. I'd written it because I thought I was in love with him, and it was the first time in my life when I felt reciprocated in energy and affections and I wanted to celebrate it. But I soon suspected it might have had an impact on Bill, and not a favourable one.

He picked me up at the airport and greeted me with a kiss on the cheek, which I found strange. Arriving at his flat in Kilburn, he said he'd let me have his bedroom and he'd move to the spare room. I found that even stranger but didn't ask anything. Although I'd bet the look on my face showed all the questions I had not the nerve to ask, but we carried on with this game of misunderstanding and pretence. It was only when I leaned against him on the sofa and he physically moved away that I realised I'd either made a terrible mistake or fallen victim to a complete asshole. Either way I was really upset. Whilst leaning against his unresponsive arm I just sort of lid down horizontally. I felt like a fool and just stayed lying down, inert, heartbroken and wondering how I'd get out of this muddle. I had just arrived and the prospect of spending 4 weeks with this guy who I thought liked me romantically but was now giving me the cold shoulder was suddenly too heavy a burden. Luckily, I had met some of his friends on the first few days, one of which was Lori, an Irish girl I got on very well with. She shared a house with 3 other girls and said I could stay there instead. Lori seemed unsurprised at Bill's attitude and told me he'd started seeing this other girl called Marcella. I was shocked, but part of me wondered if he wasn't mad. Why invite me over to then humiliate me like that? I remembered how, in the first few days of my stay he'd mention this Marcella often to his friends whenever I was close enough to hear it, as if wanting me to get what he didn't have the courage to say.

When I told Bill that I was moving to Lori's he was annoyed, but I didn't care. I think he didn't want our private affairs circulating amongst his friends, and my leaving had done just that. But given that he'd pretty much dumped me before I arrived, I felt I didn't owe him anything. I was angry and at the same time I was certain I'd totally spooked him with my candy-floss love letter, which was the probable reason for his behaviour. I reckoned I might as well have fun for the remainder of my time in London and these Irish girls certainly knew how to do that. I met some more Irish people, who all seemed to know each other and congregate around Kilburn and Hampstead. I was surprised at the mammoth nights out these people could have. They thought nothing of spending £50 in one night, which normally included drinks, club entry and cab fare back. And some sort of drug consumption inside the club. The first time we all went out Bill actually came along, as we were playing the 'no hard feelings' game to a tee. I had finally met the famous Marcella, who was a pretty girl of a VERY big size. He didn't seem that interested in her either. At last I had confirmation he'd just set out to find anyone to go out with before my arrival. It was a bitchy thing to think, that because Marcella was fat he wasn't interested. But I was in a bitchy mood and no one was going to stop me. That night at the club I made a beeline for one of their Irish friends, Seamus, who I spent almost the entire evening snogging in a corner. At this point my behaviour was not solely designed to spike Bill, but I mostly wanted to have some fun and leave behind the feeling of dread I'd carried from his rejection. Someone tripped over our feet mid snog and I realise it was Bill, who I suspected had been looking for us. I saw shock in his eyes, which made me feel a bit ashamed of my behaviour. But hang on, you betrayed me first so why should you care who I'm with? I thought. An eye for an eye.

Maybe I doomed the relationship from the moment I slammed my heart open with a letter. But I don't like to think that telling the truth of how we feel lands us in hot water. I was inexperienced and didn't know any better. What it did do though, was prevent me from ever doing it again in such a free and fearless manner. Because my letter was a waterfall of emotion, and many years later, in London, I met Bill again, whilst out with Lori, who I also hadn't seen in years. I finally asked him if my letter had scared him, and he said it had. But he still kept it, and I am sure that if he ever doubts himself he'll read my letter to breathe some inspiration in.

I went back to São José eventually, but this time with the firm intention of returning soon, to live in London for a while. I was certain that life in São José was a cul-de-sac and I just had to get out. I started to plan how I could make this happen and what my goal was. But the truth is, I didn't have a long term one. I knew how I would manage myself for a year or so and hoped that by the end of it I'd know what to do. I told my parents a white lie: that I had a place at the Royal College of Art to study film (which I did) and that I could get a scholarship (which I couldn't). I didn't feel bad about it because I knew I'd find a way to make this proposition come true. The whole process that had me be on a plane just after my birthday was arduous, like a spiritual birth. It was almost like I desperately desired it but didn't want to go. Maybe something was telling me that I wouldn't be back in a year or two as I'd thought. I sold my drum kit and my car – well, my dad's car actually. But he supported my decision more than my mother, who didn't want me to go. She could see my destiny outlined like my sister's, going away and moving to a faraway land.

My sister, now pregnant, having married her pen pal Bernard, had arrived in São José from Brussels a few months previously, to spend some time at home and give birth before deciding what to do. I had visited them in Belgium before going to see Bill and loved the atmosphere of the place, it was old Europe mixed with Francophone sensibilities and a dash of Moroccan culture here and there. It seemed to be a lot more sophisticated than London, but I wasn't about to betray my first love. They had a great apartment in a district called Saint Gilles, and I'd spend my days taking buses into town, swimming at the local Art Nouveau pool, enjoying the beer and the quirkiness of the locals – I could finally understand a lot about my favourite comic book character Tintin just by looking at Belgians and their way of life. But this was before my upcoming heartbreak, so I was still floating around in anticipation.

My nephew Ariel was born at the end of May, and what I felt when I first saw him I couldn't really describe, but I knew it was a new way of loving someone. The birth had been a bit tricky and the doctor had to do it by forceps delivery, which meant the baby's head was a bit elongated upwards on his first few days. It was cute, like a baby member of the Coneheads, but my mother didn't see the humour in it and nor did my sister, who had more than a bit of a temper and gave the doctors an earful. But his head reverted back to normal soon and so did the family mood. That baby was everything to us in the first few months, I never got bored of holding him or playing with him, and he was a super giggly child. My mother described how she felt about her first grandson: it was like having a son, but the love was even doubled, and lighter because she wasn't responsible for this little being. I was happy to see my sister looking settled with her new family, but it was only a matter of time before they left for New Zealand again. And I was the one who left first.

My departure was a whirlwind and I don't remember much, maybe I tried to drown out the sudden fear that overtook me. This would be the first time I launched myself out there into the world and the unknown. Because once the savings were gone I'd have to find a way to create my own resources. Up until now I'd had a pretty sheltered existence, with my parents giving me everything. Now I could feel the difference. I had arranged to stay at Lori's for the first few months, which worked out pretty well. I shared a house in Queen's Park with her, her sister Nuala and a Liverpudlian girl called Mary. They were all office workers or secretaries and lived typical Londoner youth lives. Work and commute all week, get hammered on Friday and possibly Saturday, spend Sunday with tea, TV and a hangover. It took me a bit of time to adapt to this lifestyle, if I ever did; I was plotting how to start working on films and looking around me and everywhere for any opportunities available. The RCA placement never materialized, and I had to start from scratch. I followed more than a few dead ends. In the end, Mary knew someone who knew a graduation student from the National Film and TV School who was directing his final film and needed someone to do continuity. She offered to connect us, and I jumped at the chance to work at the film school where people like Ridley Scott and Alan Parker had studied.

I met the producer, a lady called Annette, at a café in Camden Town. I must have been very enthusiastic because I got the job. There wasn't much to it, it was 4 weeks work for no pay and expenses and food only. But I didn't care, this was more than I'd achieved in years playing shit gigs on the wrong side of the tracks. But the one issue with my new position was that I'd never done continuity before. I thought it would be dead easy because I'd always had photographic memory and was very good with faces. And I loved English literature. How hard could it be? There was only a slight cloud hanging over my joy, which was that I'd actually lied to Annette when she asked me if I had any experience. I came up with some tall tale, telling myself I'd know what to do on the day and she'd never know. I was wrong, of course. My first day on set was a thing of wonder, like I stepped onto a magical land. I'd never seen acting other than on a TV or cinema screen. I had seen a few plays in São José, but this was something different, it was acting that engaged me. Looking back though, I probably wasn't qualified to tell whether it was good or bad acting, but just seeing cameras capture a performance kept me in a sort of trance. But reality hit pretty soon, once I realised exactly what continuity work involved.

Director and producer soon saw the truth behind my act: and that was that I didn't know what I was doing. But since it was too late in the day to find someone else, someone who could work for free, not complain and even be so enthusiastic as to offer help to other departments, they kept me on. Someone told me the basics of the job, and once I knew what I had to do I actually proved to be pretty good at it. It was true, I had photographic memory. Even now, writing this chapter, I can see people's faces, the set, and things that happened, like a film playing in my mind. It all seemed incredibly slick and professional to me, how a film set was run. Except it wasn't, but I couldn't know that on my very first job. It was a good way to start and I made a lot of friends on freebies. But the reality of subsistence started to snap me into finding paid work. London rents cost a lot more than Brazil. Anything would have cost a lot more than what I was used to, so it was the calling to grow up which I had missed so far. I recalled a

Brazilian friend who'd mentioned a restaurant in East London where she'd always found work in between her travels, and recommended I go there.

I remember the first time I walked into the North South restaurant, near the City road roundabout, on the borders of King's Cross and the oldest areas of London, Clerkenwell and the City. It was small and cosy, and the only macrobiotic restaurant in London. I didn't know much about it but was aware it was more to do with diet and lifestyle. The manager, Beata, was a Serbian girl with plaits, and flowers in her hair. There were other Serbians and Croats working there, because this being 1993 and during the Yugoslav wars, there were a lot of refugees arriving in the UK. Maybe that's why she was so willing to give me a job without a second thought. Although it wouldn't be as a waitress to start with: I was employed as a cleaner, but I was thankful for any work at this point. In Brazil my family had cleaners hired for general housework, once or twice a week. Now I was about to find out what sort of life they had. I'd have to get there before the restaurant opened, so around 7am. On cold autumn mornings I'd get up at 530am, have something to eat and get the underground to Farringdon. The caretaker let me into the empty restaurant, I'd hang up my second-hand fake fur coat and put on an apron. It was simple work, sweeping, mopping and cleaning the aluminium surfaces and work tops. I'd do the work lost in my own thoughts but appreciating the absolute silence which was only disturbed by the rasping sound of mice. And the occasional IRA bomb. One of which did go off near Moorgate in the early 1990s. But I wasn't politicized at all in those days, and just assumed it was a very bad exhaust somewhere.

It wasn't edifying work, but it was therapeutic enough, as I normally put on some of their meditation eastern music whilst I scrubbed the tables. I did this work for a few weeks, until one day one of the waiting staff didn't turn up and they offered me the job. There wasn't much waiting to be done, only work behind the counter, manning the till and washing dishes. Oh, and draw up the big black board with menu details every day, which I loved doing. There was only one menu served at lunch, and it came in big bain-maries from the kitchen upstairs. It was normally brown rice, some protein, beans or chick peas, veg and salad. People would order small or large and that was all we served, apart from challenging desserts like azuki bean mousse or tofu cheesecake. There was one particularly potent bean salad, which we called 'Turbo' because of the flatulent mist that spread over the restaurant after lunch. The clientele, mostly a bunch of faithful hippies, plus any office worker from the vicinity, would drop in every day, in search of a healthy meal. Or people who came in to the yoga centre next door and needed a pick-me-up.

Then one day one of the chefs didn't turn up and in desperation the manager asked if any of us could cook. I said yes – not only could I definitely do it, but I could also add a bit more flavour to their bland menu. I spent a few weeks just copying recipes which were favourites, so I couldn't get too creative, except for adding herbs and spices. Then the stray chef returned, but I didn't want to return to the counter. Cooking was more fun, and we also earned more money per hour. I convinced the management to keep me on as dessert chef, which was a bit of a challenge. I could not use eggs, sugar, flour or dairy on anything, so I carried on making a couple of their best sellers, but also researching some new recipes with what I could use. Macrobiotics might also be called vegan today, but they are stricter. No potatoes, tomatoes or aubergines could be used, because they carry on growing during the night, I was told, so they carry *yin* energy. I thought this was basically BS but didn't risk voicing my opinion. But I got quite good at doing the usual desserts, especially a tofu cheesecake which I expanded to include fresh pineapple. Big hit downstairs. One day I decided to do an avocado pudding which my mother loved. I called it *Sorpresa Tricolore* because it was a sort of triple coloured dessert in a glass, like an ice cream. It had avocado cream, coconut cream and carob paste. I hated carob, a cheat version of chocolate, like chicory coffee, so I eventually replaced it with strawberries. The dessert now resembled the Italian flag colours, which wasn't intentional, but I let the clientele believe it was.

It went down quite well for a bit but then it reached a plateau – apart from the fact that I'd had a couple of accidents in the kitchen while making it. I kept forgetting to click shut the blender and found myself and the kitchen walls covered in green paste. Management claimed I'd birthed a great dessert which wasn't covering its high costs so far, so back came the boring cous cous cakes.

North South was a great employer, and interesting creative people kept coming in to work, and out to do their own thing, like a conveyor belt. I'd been there for over a year and a bit, and it was perfect for the times I had voluntary film work for a couple of weeks. I could always come back to the same job, and we were encouraged to take home any left-over food at the end of the day, which was usually plenty to feed my entire household. I was still living with the Irish girls, but feeling a bit disconnected from them. They had a big house party once, like with proper dancing and open garden. By that stage I was pretty much over Bill, who'd taken on a sort of aggrieved/ indifferent stance towards me, even though he turned up at the party late and actually went up to my room when I was almost asleep. I saw him open the door and realised he might have come up for a reconciliation of sorts, which never happened in the end. Ships passing in the night, I guessed. But I was far more interested in Frank, another Irish young man who had been hanging out with us. I quickly realised the Irish can be a bit tribal, mostly spending time with each other. Irish men ended up going back to their childhood sweethearts even if they were strongly inclined to play the field for a while.

This being the early 1990's, there were plenty of opportunities for going out to clubs and raves over weekends. I was invited to join the Irish gang on a club night out which Frank was also attending – with his girlfriend. Seamus, the other bloke I'd snogged at a club, was kept safe with his girlfriend, away from the clutches of a South American vixen (me). It was one of those clubs with lots of different rooms and ambiences where people could chill, dance, smoke and snog peacefully. One of the girls in our group, a cheeky brunette called Sheila, offered me an E, which was basically a tablet of Ecstasy, a very *en vogue* recreational drug back then. My usual alarm against drugs didn't ring at all. I figured it would be a way to have fun without worrying too much about anything. Besides, I was safe with them, Sheila reassured me. So, I took it.

It was a very trippy experience. I must have taken something pretty strong, because the whole place kept changing energy. At times I had the very vivid impression that, like Dante in the Divine Comedy, I was being guided across the club by Virgil in the shape of Sheila, especially as she held my hand as we descended a spiral staircase, where lots of exhausted clubbers sat looking like the lost souls of Purgatory in Gustave Dore's engravings. She was good to her word and really looked after me, which I was grateful for after we'd left. But we stayed on until the early hours, and my last memory of the place was dancing around on the main dance floor and suddenly starting to see the place filling up with dwarves dressed in bondage, their faces covered in what appeared to be green Play Doh. I freaked out a bit, thinking my trip was going awry, but Sheila later told me that the club management had hired dwarves in bondage because it was Halloween. Nobody mentioned the green stuff, which must have been my own hallucination. I kept having flashbacks of that evening for days and even weeks after. It WAS fun, but I was a bit spooked by how all control had been taken away from me by a brain chemical that night and thought that once was probably enough. I had tried it and was done with it.

My house share with the Irish girls was about to end. At the restaurant, I'd met a slightly mad but fun Brazilian woman called Cleide, who introduced me to her friend Arnaldo, who was looking for a flatmate. He was a member of a Housing co-op, which in the mid 1990s was a very popular way to source cheaper housing. It was either that or squatting, which I had no inclination for. It had not yet been made illegal, but squatting meant no security, probably no heating and the risk of eviction was a daily menace. The co-op offered temporary accommodation, but it was never less than 12 months until a property needed to be vacated and they usually offered 4-weeks-notice and also another place to live. It was a system which worked brilliantly for my first years of relative penury in London. It was also a healthy way to use up empty properties and keep them from squatters, which was a bit ironic given I'd met a few. But I liked the safety of my own home, even if it was a bit of a dump. It was also far cheaper than my single room in Queen's Park.

The first apartment I shared with Arnaldo was a dump indeed. It was on a tower block not far from expensive Kensington, on the outskirts of Ladbroke Grove and Portobello Road. It had no heating, so we had to buy a huge gas heater, with cannisters that were replaced by a supplier. It was a highly unattractive but necessary piece of furniture, and it stank of gas sometimes. I'm sure it wasn't terribly safe, but who were we to complain? I wasn't earning that much at the restaurant because I was taking more time off to work on school graduation film projects. But I still managed to buy some bits and pieces for the new home, which was after all my first proper home, even if still shared. There was a separate toilet, but the bath itself was in the kitchen, covered by a wooden board. The first time I saw it I couldn't get my head around it – how could anyone clean themselves in the kitchen? It was like being back in 1850. It wasn't even a shower – I had to buy a cheap shower head to have anything resembling what I'd been used to in Brazil. I wondered if I'd ever manage to have a shower and fry an egg at the same time. I didn't find the situation funny enough to even try. But people get used to shit environments, and after a while, so did we.

Arnaldo was a quiet guy, gay, with a massive collection of scarves, and kept himself to himself, which I quite liked. We both agreed that the sitting room was covered in hideous mismatched chintzy wall paper, but we lacked the money or energy to do anything about it. This was the problem with temporary accommodation: because the deadline was fluid, it was not worth spending time or effort on changing much. Sometimes I think back to those days with nostalgia mixed with mild horror at how I could live in a place like that. It would be many years before I found more permanent lodgings I was happy with, and it makes me wonder if it wasn't a self-fulfilling prophecy. I didn't want to be tied down by anything in my first years in London, and that was exactly what I got – no certain job, boyfriend or home. There was a sense of bohemian vagary which I enjoyed. There was also my recurring sense of artists needing to endure some sort of hardship to produce any art worth exhibiting. Thinking about this now makes me cringe a bit, given that over the years my views on art and creativity have taken a 180° turn. Here I was, around 30 years old, trying to find my way in the world, and going down a road which would not change much until about 7 years later.

A friend from São José, Yara, lived in a big corner house almost opposite our building. She was married to popstar ____ ____then, and they had a young child. I had met Yara back in Brazil when she was dating my friend Edson Z, a guitarist from Brasilia. They stayed in our house once while touring with their band Shit Life, and Yara would tag along. We had a game of leaving blank paper on a type writer and people would sit and write stuff to which others replied throughout the days they stayed there. Before smart phones and internet we certainly knew how to have lots of fun… Now she was settled in London, and we got to spend some time with her socially. My other friend Carla had just arrived from São José and was staying there, working as an au pair. I met ____ ____ a few times, and they had a couple of very cool parties there, where I will forever remember we shared drinks with the late Joe Strummer and other notorious pop heroes.

I was asked to house sit for them once, while they travelled to Brazil and Europe, and I was relieved to leave my poxy flat for a bit of luxury for a while. I even shot (and acted in) a short film there, which I never told Yara. My first and only job as an actress, directed by Francesca, an Italian girl I'd met at the National Film School. It was good training to be in front of a camera though, because I got to feel what an actor goes through. It is a vulnerable space, and it made me appreciate acting even more when I became a director myself.

When the co-op gave us the customary 4-weeks-notice I realised it was time to go solo, and so did Arnaldo. We got on OK but both of us knew we were just too different and had very little in common. I got offered a studio flat – a bedsit, actually – near Gray's Inn Road and Bloomsbury, which was a part of London with lots of history. Not only the Pre-Raphaelite brotherhood, but also the Bloomsbury set of Virginia Woolf and the Bell sisters had had homes nearby. There was also a whole trail left by Charles Dickens, who had lived two blocks away in the 1850s. For a history and literature buff like me it was the perfect spot. I lived upstairs from Ishree, an Eritrean lady who had been a refugee in the 1980s. She once told me some crazy stories about her past life as a princess who had to escape her country on horseback. She must have suffered greatly, because even if I knew nothing about PTSD, I could detect clear signs of it. But she was the kindest neighbour I ever had. When I was ill with the flu for 3 days, she turned up at my door with a tray of soup and bread, telling me off for not asking for help. There was also an old Italian lady next door who was quite mothering, which gave me some degree of succour, being so far from my own family.

I'd sometimes get some fun gigs via my old journalist contacts in Brazil. I was asked to go to the premiere of the film *Chaplin*, directed by Richard Attenborough and starring Robert Downey Jr. Later on, I went to the Ritz Hotel in Piccadilly to interview director and star. I couldn't believe my luck. There was a press reception on arrival and I simply stuffed myself with canapes and champagne until we were called upstairs in groups of 3. First up was Lord Dickie (as he was affectionately called), who was the most delightful man – he was so nice it would have been hard to write a bad word about his film. I knew I wasn't kidding anyone about being a journalist, but they bought my act, given I had a daily press permit. Another assignment was more exciting to me: the press release of Duran Duran's new album, at a posh hotel in Holland Park. I was totally star struck as I'd spent my teens lusting after those chiselled faces, except they looked a bit ravaged by excess and extravagance. And Roger Taylor wasn't there. But there were canapes and champagne again. I thought I could make a part-time living out of this, but once I found out I hadn't been paid for my article on *Chaplin* I ditched my press pass.

It was whilst I lived at ___ Street that I got my first accountant and agent. Things were starting to look up on the employment front. I had done a couple of feature films outside the film school orbit, which paid peanuts but at least it was something. I had met a whole crew of people on a dreadful film called Rabid Zeus, which nevertheless was fun to work on. It was a horror/ sci fi based on the tired premise that a group of chancers dock on an abandoned science research station near Crete, only to find there was a mutating panther that adapted to human genomes...It was one of the first films to be shot on the former war bunker and now super busy Long Hill studios on the outskirts of London. I met a lot of people who stayed in my life for a few years afterwards, and who followed me onto the next job, both produced by a man some considered a hero, others a villain. His name was Saul, and he always worked with another producer called Saul as well. We called them The Two Sauls. I guess we were paid a pittance, but their gigs were the most fun I'd had so far.

After Rabid Zeus, the Two Sauls got me a gig on their new film Right and Proper, which was to be a parody of the Merchant Ivory films about Edwardian England. It was a long shoot but probably the most fun I ever had on a film set. We had 4 weeks in the Isle of Man, 5 weeks in India and 2 weeks in Italy. Douglas was the capital of the Isle of Man and one of the most boring places I'd ever been to. I might have a completely different idea if I returned there now: it was possible to cross the whole island by car, in every direction, in 45 minutes, and there was something about fairies on a bridge. It was known for its annual motorbike race and a breed of cats with no tail. We shot the British part of the film, which features an upper-class English family who go abroad but never lose their Empire ways, much in the vein of Room with A View and Howards End. By the time we left for India we were all thick as thieves and almost best friends. Working on films can do that to people. We spend almost 14 hours a day together, in a high-pressure environment, 5 and sometimes 6 days per week. Friendships bonded, and romances blossomed, sometimes with dire consequences if one of the parties was married or betrothed to someone else. I had a crush on the line producer, a guy called Aidan, who had a serious alcohol problem, a small detail I was unaware about until our wrap party in India. I'd had a one-night-stand with Jackson, one of the assistant directors on Rabid Zeus, but by the time we met again it was all in the past and he was eyeing up one of the make-up girls – who also seemed keen. I then started to get the hots for an Indian art department assistant called Inderjit, but fortunately it was towards our last week in India, or I might have got myself into trouble. This was the sort of dynamics that went on during that shoot.

My time in India is something I will never forget, even if I never return to that amazing country. It is said that India is such an awakening of the senses that there are just two reactions to it: love or hate. I went for the first one. I'd never seen so much poverty and so much beauty in the same spot, and I thought I'd seen it all in Brazil. India is different; it bewitches you to find beauty where you normally would not. The first place we saw was Mumbai (called Bombay back in the 1990s), which was a direct assault on the senses the minute we stepped off the plane. We were taken on a four-hour bus journey up the mountains to a tea growing region called Ootacamund, on the Nilgiri Hills. I will forever remember the old 1950s bus snaking up the steep mountains from Coimbatore, where the weather was oppressively hot, and as we climbed higher and higher the mist started to cover the hills and the damp air gave the palm trees and hibiscus flowers a translucent shine. We stopped at a roadside kiosk where the biggest sellers were banana crisps and Fanta, and the owners greeted us like pop stars. We had to make a stop later for toilet breaks, except there were no toilets, and I had to crouch next to our main British star, trying to shelter her pissing from prying eyes, which turned out to be over-excited monkeys screeching round a roadside temple, as if to disrupt some heathen prayer.

We were to be joined in Ootacamund by the film's big star, Sir ____ _____. It turns out he didn't like being called 'Sir' and was a born comedian, albeit the most erudite funny man I'd ever seen. He spoke 10 languages fluently and used to entertain us for hours at dinner at the posh country hotel we were all staying at, telling us incredible stories from his past shoots. In our film he was playing an old colonial aristocrat who still dreamed of the Raj (the British Empire in India) and had a crush on the spinster aunt character. He once played a trick on the assistant directors by finishing a scene under the bath water and failing to emerge, which sent frazzled runners off to get a medic and possibly an ambulance. But he'd been hiding under water on purpose and burst back up laughing. He spoke to me in Portuguese once, having found out I was Brazilian. Never, before or since, was an actor so open and interested enough in who I was/am to find out how to say some words in my language. He was a total gentleman, of the sort that has become extinct a long time ago.

When I think of India now, I wonder if it was all just a dream. While still in Brazil the only time I was exposed to anything to do with the Indian culture was when the local highbrow Culture Network showed the British series Jewel in The Crown, which I was mesmerized by. I've since worked with two of its stars (Geraldine James and Art Malik) and often see Charles Dance, who played officer Guy Perron, shopping at my local supermarket. He is still a majestic presence, even with children running around him. But in Ootacamund and the Nilgiri Hills we were also running around like kids, drinking the atmosphere, going to religious festivals where the locals daubed our foreheads with a dot of red powder as a sign of respect for Ganesh. On the way back, we took a bus up the mountains to our hotel, deciding in a moment of madness to travel on the roof of the bus like so many Indians did. We stood tall, mock-surfing on the roof as the bus made its way up the bends, breathlessly crouching down when a huddle of power cables zoomed into us, throwing frantic shadows over the dusty track on an endless moonlit night. Thinking back, I am sure I had my guardian angel working overtime to keep me safe.

During the shoot we entered villages within the tea plantations which were kept working like a feudal system, and yet everyone looked really happy. Hordes of young children would welcome us, looking in wonder at our skin colour and touching us, making me think they'd never seen white people before. Poor people, who seemed to possess not much beyond a home and each other, also looked radiant, with their dazzling white smiles, clothes made out of simple but lovely fabrics, and garlands of flowers and jewellery cascading down hair and necks – even young children. I could feel a lot of love emanating from them and it was a revelation. Even when

I had to find a toilet in the middle of a tiny village, as I was coming down with the unavoidable 'Delhi belly' or its more extreme cousin 'Madras madness', on entering the cubicle I found an old woman in a pink saree holding a golden jug who welcomed me with near reverence. It was like being in an Aesop fable, or having to solve a riddle as price of entry. I will never forget that toilet: it was a rectangular small white washed building with open windows which were just holes. Inside, there were cubicles with no doors, in which I had to squat over a hole in the ground. The smell was indescribable, and there were flies everywhere. I didn't have time to negotiate my movements as whatever was in my tummy was coming down fast, but luckily the old woman had presented me with a jug of water, as there were no toilet tissues anywhere. It was almost a mystical experience, making me acutely aware, like St Thomas Aquinas, that we are born through a channel located between piss and poo, and it may be a clue to the transience of life.

Indians seemed to face this predicament with an almost zen tranquillity. Any exterior shooting had us presented with the same dilemma, because Delhi belly was slowly taking us over in waves. One of the Indian location managers built a wooden structure around a hole in the ground on top of a hill, with black drapes covering the sides. This was our toilet for the day. But because the monsoon was just around the corner, sometimes a gust of wind would blow the drapes as some unfortunate victim of Delhi belly was just about to relieve themselves. I don't know how many times I took a dump in the bushes, just to avoid the embarrassing spectacle of having my bottom hanging out on a hill. I was actually properly ill for a couple of days, which I mostly spent in the toilet in my room. I'd had sunstroke the day before, and our unit nurse could predict what was coming. I had to quickly ask Tara, the director's assistant, to replace me for a couple of days. She'd never script supervised anything, but was very clever and fast thinking, and with some markers from me she managed to keep the ship afloat.

The last leg of our shoot was a doddle, by comparison. We were staying in a Rome suburb called Latina, which was near Cisterna, both founded by Benito Mussolini in 1932 to house people coming from other regions to work in Rome. The local Italian crew told us they were both nicknamed Latrine and Cistern due to their association with fascism. By the time we made it there it was just a sleepy, if anodyne neighbourhood with some decent hotels and coffee shops, but the best thing about it was the train station right next to our hotel, which took us to Rome in less than 30 minutes. We shot scenes in the main Roman landmarks Campo Marzio, Colosseum and Spanish Steps, with some interiors around old Roman villas with all the wonderful clichés they entailed. I had the sense that I'd need to return to Rome many times, to fully experience all this city had to reveal. The shoot also took us to a garden complex just outside Rome, called Ninfa. It is one of the most beautiful places I've ever seen. It helped that we were there around spring, so all the flowers and trees were in bloom. The entire garden was like something out of a dream, or an impressionist painting. I've often wanted to return there, but perhaps I would be trying to reproduce a spiritual snapshot which will forever be encased in my memory.

Returning to London, I went back to my studio flat, where my friend Chloe had been living during my absence. Not long after that I got another move notice from the co-op, so I had to pack up fairly quickly. Steve and Hannah, who I'd met recently on shoots and were to become firm friends for a number of years, agreed to help me pack a van with my belongings for my next home, which was to be in Cricklewood, an old Irish neighbourhood not far from Lori and Bill, who I now rarely saw. It was a bit nicer, and with a separate bedroom and living room, even if on the small side. There was a little terrace outside via the back door, but I soon found out there was a risk of getting a bowl of dirty water thrown down by the African matriarch upstairs, if I dared stand there too long. I considered complaining, but since I'd only just moved in, I didn't want a fight with a neighbour. Turns out being offered that flat was a mistake by the co-op and I had to prepare my move again. Carla had been staying with me for a while as she was looking for an alternative to Yara's house, which she compared to 'modern slavery'. The co-op then offered us a 2-bedroom house just around the corner from ____ Street, which was an area I loved, and so we agreed to share it. Just before we moved out of Cricklewood, Carla got the news that her mum had died. I was with her and was happy to be of some comfort. I hugged her tight for a long time, and she said she'd had the feeling she was hugging her mum. It would not be the last time I'd have a sort of shamanic experience: just before my grandmother

Helena passed away the following year, I sat with her in hospital when she was in a great deal of pain in her back. Wanting to relieve her pain, I concentrated on healing and put my hands across her spine, and gently massaged her up and down. I don't know what I did, but it worked, and I will never forget her hands pressing mine in gratitude.

We moved to _____ Street, which was a late Georgian house with 2 bedrooms and a garden. We couldn't believe our luck. The previous tenant was an old Italian lady who had recently passed away and left most of her old furniture and crockery intact. We were at Clerkenwell's doorstep, which had a proud tradition of Italian immigrants and delis nearby. Most of the houses and flats around us were council, which means they were owned and run by local government. This would have meant that a big chunk of London consisted of cheaper social housing, which has changed a lot since the late 1990s. From where we lived, up until the areas around King's Cross Station, it was all a bit derelict and definitely still carrying the whiff of a Dickensian past. I remember going to a New Year's Rave at a big Victorian warehouse, probably a coal deposit back in the 1850s but now, like most similar buildings in the environs, it had fallen into disrepair. The whole perimeter around the station and St Pancras was a bit scary at night, a favourite playground for drug addicts and prostitutes. There was something about this penury which I found very literary and inspiring. Sometimes I felt as if I was embedded within the Tales of Two Cities universe.

Our new house didn't need much, and I was happy with the room I picked. We never did much about the garden, which was permanently overgrown with lots of fading sunflowers and a network of slug trails on the patio stones, which glinted in the sun whenever we ventured outside. I remember where I was in the house when news of my favourite grandmother's death came in, leaving me inconsolably sat on the steps leading to the garden. At that moment I actually felt her presence next to me. There was something warm and soothing enveloping my entire back, and I knew it was HER.

The house was a welcoming place for sorrow and joy. I'd started dating George, a bassist who played with a Goth-lite type band which was actually quite good. It was a relationship which started without the usual drama and procrastination I'd experienced previously. He was nice and fun, and it was sexually fulfilling as well – except for the following mornings. George had coccydynia, which meant tailbone pain as soon as he got out of bed. He was on painkillers the entire morning and it was a bit of a dampener on our romance. The other issue with George was that he didn't like commitment of any sort – even arranging to have a coffee later in the day made him a bit jittery. This was before mobile phone use became widespread, but I already had one. George had a 'number', a landline that I could call and leave a message in case there was something urgent to say. I think I tried it a couple of times, but my messages never got through to him. It was a case of him contacting me whenever he wanted, but that rule did not apply to me. He might as well have been an FBI informer. I was getting a bit tired of this one-sided affair, but we both dragged it on for another year.

Before I met George, I got an offer to work on an Italian movie in Morocco. A director I'd worked with on a BBC adaptation of Jane Austen's *Pride and Prejudice* recommended me to production. They called me and tried to hire me, but I'd have to pay for my ticket to Morocco. Even back then, with my relatively short CV, I thought that was a ludicrous proposition and refused. They relented, and offered me £600 per week, which was pretty low, but I'd never been to Morocco and the sense of adventure lured me. I remembered the amazing times I'd had in India for a lower salary and decided it was worth it. The script was in English, but most of the crew were Italian. I had a bit of a rude awakening. We arrived in Marrakesh and changed planes to Ouarzazate, which was a Moroccan version of an early Hollywood studio. They put us up at the Atlas Hotel, which had an imposing façade with tall walls, like a fortress – only for the illusion to be shattered once we went in the gates and realised the walls stopped just as they bent round the building, like one of these fake cowboy movie sets. It was like an omen for the entire shoot.

Some of the Italians were rude and prejudiced against anyone who wasn't white, or more importantly, Italian. The catering team were of a similar disposition, organising the queues by skin tone: whites first, followed by Moroccans, and blacks last. Even being white didn't ensure good service, as it largely depended on the chef's mood; if it was bad, it was expected that some amount of pasta would land on someone's head. The French sound team staged a protest but were relegated to the back of the queue as punishment, behind the poor black extras. And these people had been brought over from Senegal to be in the film, which was meant to be set in South Africa during the Boer War. Most of them were highly educated students looking for a bit of adventure and cash - not to be enslaved in real life! When they were made to spend most of the morning down at an old iron ore mine with no masks, water of food, some of the British crew issued an ultimatum to the producer, a Mafioso-looking smooth-talking Roman called Matteo de Angelis. I think he buckled under pressure and sent some ADs down with food and water. Matteo could be funny and horrible, often at the same time. His nephew Lucca was the entirely incompetent location manager (in charge of things like making sure locations were easily accessible, which almost never happened), and to me, clearly the name de Angelis was full of sound and fury. They once forgot our lead actor's trailer (with him napping inside) in the middle of the desert, and the poor man awoke to see the sunset and tumbleweed whistling around him.

When the company was about to move to a trendy beach resort frequented in the past by Orson Welles and the Rolling Stones, Matteo told me my services were no longer required by the director. There were 3 days with lots of dialogue to be shot and I wondered if he'd gone insane with sunstroke. But that was his decision and there was nothing I could do. Until I discovered there were no plans to get me to Casablanca; they were just going to leave me there to make my way to the airport! I was going to make a scene, but the costume department convinced me to shut up and tag along and offered me a bed in one of their rooms. I thought I might as well just go with them and have a holiday until the departure date. On the first shoot date I watched from a distance and noticed the director looking daggers at me. Later, at the hotel, he asked me why I didn't turn up for work. I think I tried to tell him about his mad producer but by this stage I'd had enough of their corrupt working ethics and decided to have some fun with the Brits. That night someone gave me some hashish to smoke and I almost blacked out. I simply do not remember how I got to my bed or what I did after the first few drags. I had my guardian angel to thank for, once again, keeping me safe in the face of spiritual and practical corruption.

I've not been back to Morocco since, but I loved it. Trips to Kasbahs and rose festivals, hammam spas with women of all ages, who curiously stared at our body hair as if we'd come from another planet. I once saw two teenage girls reclined on top of one another, in the middle of the hammam, and while one of the girls hummed softly, the other shaved her friend's pubic hair with loving attention. It was a scene of such erotic innocence that even the Victorian painter Alma Tadema might not have known how to do it justice. Morocco was full of such moments. I once had a marriage proposal from a young runner who asked me for a lift from our hotel to the production office – I'd been allowed to drive their crappy hired Fiats. I can't remember his name, but I'd noticed him looking at me on set whenever I had a moment for myself. And now, driving in the cool and starry Ouarzazate night, I listened to a crescendo of his cries of affection until he said he loved me. I tried to play it cool, offering some older woman wisdom back. He didn't know me at all, and he couldn't possibly mean it. But the vehemence of his obvious passion struck a chord within me; no man had ever spoken to me of love in my 32 years, at least not with such eloquence, and here was this young kid telling me what I'd longed to hear from other lips in my past. Right moment, right feeling, wrong man. It had to be an exact equation though, and I had to disappoint this eager young lover.

Back in London, I'd barely had time to digest my Moroccan experiences before I got an offer to work in the Galapagos Islands. This would mean returning to Ecuador, which I'd longed to do for years. It was a drama documentary about a 1940s scientist who followed in Darwin's footsteps. It was a really cool job, with us spending two weeks in the main islands, filming such wonderful beasts of nature, who seemed undisturbed by the frantic rigmarole film crews create around them. I didn't have time to visit Guayaquil or my friend Mariangela, who I had not heard of for years. But recently I'd found out she was living in Paris, having married a French scientist. After Ecuador I found my parents waiting for me in London, looked after by Carla and another friend. We had a family trip booked to Italy, where we would retrace some of the steps of the original patriarch Benedetto Colleoni.

I didn't go back to Brazil during my first three years in England. I remember getting some hurt letters from my father, weaving tales of emotional abandonment. It was strangely true. I had been so housebound my entire childhood and adolescence, that it was indeed odd for me to disappear and go out of communication. This wasn't to do with my parents. It was simply the huge relief I felt to be out of an atmosphere that had become almost spiritually oppressive to me. Even in relative poverty and away from all the comforts I had been accustomed to, I felt much freer. There's an expression in Portuguese which goes something like 'eating bread kneaded by the Devil.' It means experiencing extreme hardship. That hadn't been my case because if push came to shove, I could always go back to Brazil. I had definitely licked some crumbs of it though. The first time I returned was pretty emotional. I felt guilt, elation, happiness, longing, all rolled into one amorphous ball of feeling. I spent two months with my parents and suddenly didn't want to go back to London. I felt protected and nurtured like I hadn't for a whole three years. My mother was quite happy for me to stay on, and surprisingly it was my father's voice of reason that prevailed. He said: do you really want to run back to the nest and leave your dreams behind? I knew he was right, and I also knew he would support me whenever I needed it.

The next time I saw them was when we travelled to Italy, which was another emotional journey – for my mother especially. Retracing her grandparents' steps and birth places in Lombardia. I encountered part of my roots there and marvelled at how similar to Italians our attitudes and reactions to the world were. I was relieved to see that behaviour such as the De Angelis' was probably an exception. Although I got a couple of calls from Matteo while on my next job in Paris. He wanted me to post him all my edit notes for the film, which I'd kept as ransom. They still owed me two weeks' wages, and I told him he'd get my notes once the cash landed on my account. I was probably being entirely reckless, and it didn't even cross my mind that the Mafia might come after me. But I was still furious at being left to fend for myself in the Atlas Mountains and threw caution to the wind. He never got the notes, and I am, to this day, still owed £1200.

I settled back into London life once my parents left. My next jobs would take me back to Northern Italy, the Netherlands and Somerset, where I met great people, some of whom are still good friends. Two of the jobs I did in this period presented me with a strange challenge: there was a void of leadership on set, and when I say leadership, I mean people who inspire others to follow their vision. There was none of that present. The first one was a film directed by the angriest man in the world, who alienated people with his gratuitous cruelty. The second film was actually great fun, but the director was there in body but not in spirit. His first assistant director was equally incompetent, more interested in looking good to the producers than rallying the troops. Seeing the void, I stepped into it. Along with the cinematographer, I made decisions about blocking of scenes and actors' performances. I even made him grab his camera when I saw a church surrounded by mist on top of an Italian hill, which begged to be filmed...we called the lead actor on set and he improvised some action. My shot made it into the trailer and the finished film, for which I was proud, and at the same time wondered how someone so uninterested in directing actors could get a film financed. Perhaps it had less to do with talent than I'd previously thought.

Between jobs, once more we received a notice warning from the co-op. But this time there was a shortage of housing, and we realised it might take longer than 4 weeks to find a new home. I started to think of various plan B scenarios and had an offer from my friend Steve to stay at his place for a week or so until I found alternative arrangements. On the day I was due to vacate the house, I just couldn't find Steve. He wasn't at his home and his mobile wasn't answering. I'd packed all my possessions and filled the hire car I'd been driving since my old Volvo had been broken into. I headed to South London, as I knew that's where he lived and decided to park somewhere and have a drink at a café until he called me back. It was getting dark when I finally got him on the phone. He told me he was staying at his girlfriend's place in North London, and that he wouldn't be back home for a week or so and why didn't I ring our mutual friend Bob as he was sure I would be able to stay there? I was in tears. Sat in my loaded car, at 9pm, homeless, with nowhere to go. I had the genius idea to call my friend Paula who also lived nearby, and she truly saved me. She shared a flat with 2 other girls, but she told me I could share her double bed until I found another alternative. And I had to be up at 5am the following day to go to work, so it was a gesture I wouldn't ever forget.

This turned out to be the perfect solution for a while. Once I finished the job one of the girls who shared the other room decided to leave, and so I settled in the house, sharing with another Brazilian girl. We were very different, but somehow it worked. I knew to keep myself to myself and so did she, but with a general friendly vibe. I didn't contact Steve again. He called me weeks later, as if nothing had happened, or at least making it seem like it was a minor mishap for both of us. He left me a few messages, but I couldn't bring myself to respond. I just wanted him to eff off. Until I heard his last voicemail, in which he angrily demanded to know if I was ignoring him. I think I called him and left a message confirming his suspicions. We had a bit of a stand-off about it, neither ceding territory to the other. In the end I got tired of it. We didn't speak for a long while, and later we resumed our friendship, but to me it was no longer as close as it had been. I could no longer trust him. We drifted apart years later, mainly because he was hanging out with some coke heads, and I knew what that was like from my pop star times in Brazil. I was no longer interested. I was sorry to lose his presence in my life, but I started wondering if he was indeed who I thought he was. When all else failed, my intuition kicked in.

George the tail boned bassist was still in my life. But not for long. We had one or two more encounters, which were very nice, but I remembered the frustration of never being able to track him down when he didn't want to be found. I think we drifted apart eventually. It wasn't a sudden traumatic rift. Which told me we'd gotten used to each other, rather than being united by a strong passionate bond. I met him again years later, at one of the nights out Carla organised, which usually threw together some cult pop stars, alternative rockers and fashion victims. It was good to see him, and he had fond memories of our time together. It meant something, he said. What it meant he couldn't say. He was with a girl hanging on his every word, looking very unhappy. I felt sorry for her, and grateful to the gods of romance for not having fallen for someone mentally unavailable like George again.

It was nearing the time when we would have to renew the contract for the flat, and I decided to put some pressure on the co-op about our next home. I had to keep opening the avenues of possibility, and finally they told me there was a 4-bedroom house we could move into, if I could find two more people to join in. Apart from me and Carla, there was now Paula, who was up for it, and Heike, an artist friend of Hannah's from Hamburg, who was a bit eccentric but seemed like a good fit for us. We went to see the house, an old Victorian semi in a posh area of Somers Town. It was in pretty good nick, except for the floors and some dreadful wall colours, but we could change all that. We got the floorboards sanded and the worst colours painted over, and each of us was pretty happy with the room we got – except for Carla, who had her heart set on the double room, which Paula got. The next step was to fumigate the entire house, to eliminate bad vibes and spirits of last inhabitants. This was Paula's idea. She was always a bit of a psychic and while exploring the attic she once found a big porcelain plate with a printed photograph of Alesteir Crowley on it, sat on a throne, covered with a tiger mantle. That was a bit of a freakish moment and we all agreed that the smell of burning incense for two days was a necessity.

The conviviality worked well for a few months, but cracks soon started to appear. It was a big house that needed to be cleaned often, but some people did more than others. An attempt to collect weekly money for essentials like cleaning products and toilet paper didn't go as well as expected. There was only one bathroom for 4 people, which could cause some attrition. Heike was always the early riser, so she would have the first shower. Carla took ages bathing which meant no one wanted to be next in line. Heike also liked to host dinner parties, and she did so about 3 times a week. Which irritated Paula a great deal, coming home tired and wanting a quick dinner and finding the diner and kitchen in a sort of bohemian reunion vibe. I detected all of the above and to avoid the criss crossing of 'energies', I decided to accept some work away, near Somerset and the Lake District. I spent almost two months in hotels and gorgeous locations, putting the home feuding out of my mind for at least some time. I was a bit surprised to meet Frank, the Irish friend of Lori and Sheila, working on it as cinematographer. The sparks that had flown between us in the past had never been properly investigated, and I thought this may be a good opportunity. But nothing much happened because Frank was one of those guys who play around with flirtatious energy to the max, only to disappear once it threatens to manifest. Unless I was completely mistaken and imagined the whole scenario, but it didn't seem likely. In any case, he had a girlfriend and I thought prudent to avoid heartbreak in the middle of a job as intense as this.

It was around this time that I was introduced to a personal development course which changed the direction my life was going. Paula was the one who had done it over a weekend, and I remember she called me on Sunday, it was nearly midnight, but she had such energy in her voice like I had not heard it before. She said, 'you HAVE to do the course I am doing!', to which I replied I would, because I trusted her completely. She was always into mysticism, spirituality, nutrition and natural healing, whereas I hadn't fully bought into it. Yet. But I had always felt there was more to life than this constant racing and making it somewhere. I thought there wasn't much that I didn't agree with Jesus on, and that God existed somewhere, even if it was a form of energy that inhabited me, the rain or the mice that started to make their presence felt under our floorboards. And so, it was a matter of time before I embraced a more spiritual approach to life.

Paula invited me to the completion evening for the course, and when I got there, I could feel the buzz in the air. People smiling from ear to ear, with name badges on. If I'd had an ounce of scepticism, I might have made my excuses and left, but I didn't. I actually have a highly critical character, but I just couldn't see anything wrong with so much joy surrounding me; it gave me a good feeling and also a certain hope that I'd find the tribe I only suspected I'd been looking for. I registered on the spot, although they had some smaller introductions in which the room was divided into. We got a guy who struck me as not terribly well trained, preaching to at least one converted (me), which started to annoy me somewhat. But I sensed that the real value would have been in the course itself, which was 3 full days and one evening.

My initiation into the world of New Circle was with its flagship course called the First Circle. And that's what it was in my life, a landmark. It wasn't like I'd fallen off my horse, vision impaired, on the road to Damascus (that happened on the Second Circle, 3 months later, except for the vision bit). But I was definitely and forever shifted in my perception of the world. On the Monday after the course, I felt like I'd just been released from a prison in my mind. All the things that I believed I was meant to be and do crumbled in three days. Not in a destructive way, but actually, it really was like scales had fallen off my eyes. I envisaged a present and a future in which my senses seemed to be sharper, and the listening I had for people in my life was more generous. There was some subtle magic as to how it happened. In a room full of people, about 150 souls, and a leader who spoke most of the time. She wasn't saying anything I hadn't heard before, and I deducted it was to do with the intense process of looking at life and what we make of it for 3 full days, non-stop. Also having to face moments in which I thought I was a victim of circumstances, only to uncomfortably realise I had a choice in most matters. To say it was a revelation was an understatement; it was almost like wiping an energetic slate clean. It had such an impact on me that I decided to register for the Second Circle, which left me a couple of months free to visit my sister & parents reunited in New Zealand, via a stopover in Tokyo where my friend Bonnie was living.

I didn't have much time to see it properly but what I saw of Japan made me want to return soon. No one spoke English, not even at immigration. And they all had those strange face masks for fear of viruses. The words that come to mind about Japan are 'strange' and 'amazing'. For a lapsed graphic designer like me, everything in Tokyo seemed to be made for my eyes. Or the eyes of an artist or an aesthete. Every little sign on the subway showed a word of imagination and thought behind it. The place was a cocktail of honour, humility and zaniness. And the food was to die for, but in a totally different way from Italian cooking. It was minimalistic, nourishing and perfect in every way. I could actually be describing the Japanese ethos exactly as I described their cuisine. It also seemed to me that although they exported a lot of stuff, they seemed to keep the best versions of their technology jealously reserved for internal consumption. I only stayed in Tokyo for 5 days, which does not seem like enough to have gathered all the above impressions, but I can be a sharp and focused observer, especially when I am outside my normal environment. I even made a little short film from my MiniDV footage. I wasn't thinking about it when I shot it, but I wanted to make sure I didn't miss a thing, so the camera became my eyes as I was permanently trying to shoot whatever I saw that piqued my interest.

I met my parents in Auckland, and the plan was for me to travel back to Brazil with them and spend a month there. I had been to see my sister in Auckland before, but her circumstances had changed a bit. She was separated from Bernard, and my nephew Ariel was now 8 years old. Her new partner was fellow chef Hans, and they'd had a baby the year before, my youngest nephew Billy. They had a small restaurant at the University of Auckland food court and business was apparently booming. She seemed happy even if their work schedule was punishing. I liked New Zealand a lot, with its amazing natural beauty, great weather, friendly people and prosperity. My father thought it was what Brazil could look like if it stopped electing crooks to office. He'd suffered a heart attack when my sister left, probably because hearing baby Ariel's cries as he was led into the boarding gates had an emotional impact he couldn't process, except by manifesting it on a physical level. It happened during my extended sabbatical in London, while I concentrated 100% on my career goals. I wouldn't have thought of my activities as goals in the past, although I was certainly driven. But he recovered, and here they were, happy to see my sister settled and content. We left for Brazil via Argentina, which was the most tiring trip I ever experienced. I think the three of us slept for 2 whole days after arriving. Once I got my wits about me, I received some annoying news about my new flatmates.

Our contract at the big house had come to an end yet again. This time finding a new home was much quicker, because we decided to split the household. Paula had left the house months earlier, no doubt fed up with Heike's frequent dinner parties. She found a couple of Argentinian musicians to take over her room. They were Gustavo and Mariana, an actual couple, who seemed very nice, but no one seemed to have noticed that the house population went from 4 to 5, still with one bathroom. Not including Carla's then boyfriend Greg, who was staying with us whilst his new house was being decorated. He brought his big wide screen TV with him and assumed it exonerated him from paying council tax or doing any cleaning. Things would have gotten ugly between us, but luckily he left earlier than predicted. At that point we got the co-op notice, but with good news of 2 flats available on the same block. Heike and Carla would take one, and myself and the couple would take the other flat. The news I received in Brazil made me realize I'd probably made a mistake. Because Paula needed a place to stay, I let her take my room for the month, thinking there would be no issue with Gustavo and Mariana, given that they knew each other. Halfway through my holiday I get complaints from all three, Paula saying she'd been accused of flirting with Gustavo, and Mariana saying I should have asked them before inviting Paula to stay.

In the end the issue got resolved, but there was some fighting involved. Paula eventually left England and settled in Budapest, where she built her new life and met her current husband. So, what may have seemed disempowering at the time was the route to something better. But I wasn't ready to learn that lesson yet. As I got back to London and time went by, I had conflicting impressions about my flatmates. Most times we got on very well, other times I was annoyed by their constant music playing and rehearsing in the next room, very loudly. They worked from home and I was a constant request for the music to be turned down. I didn't want to be a pain in the ass, but it seemed like there was a power struggle going on. Two against one. It wasn't an ideal situation and I started to feel trapped. I couldn't get out and get another flat, and if I did, I'd risk losing co-op membership. But then something happened which proved to be the last straw for me. Mariana and Gustavo had started hanging out with a trendy Austrian guy who looked like a cross between Frank Zappa and Beck. He was actually very funny and worked as a DJ. They went everywhere together. Until Mariana started having an affair with him and moved out for a while. Gustavo was upset, and I tried to help by having long conversations about life, love, or whatever I could think to console him a bit. The affair eventually fizzled out and she came back, and they resumed their relationship. But she noticed we were a bit chummier[9], and one day made a sarcastic remark, with the inference that I'd got a bit too close to him. I couldn't believe that this woman, who'd just semi-dumped her husband, was now – not in so many words, but still - accusing me of trying to lure/ seduce him in some way. It occurred to me that it was a déjà vu of Paula's earlier situation. I wasn't mature enough to see it at the time, but more than likely her issue was nothing to do with me. Nevertheless, it hurt me, and I decided I'd had enough, even if it meant leaving my own home behind.

But before all this brouhaha came about, I met someone who would become a significant relationship in my life – at least for a while. I was still participating in New Circle courses. It kept possibility alive and I met lots of great people during the various courses I took. It was what kept hope in humanity afloat when 9/11 happened and helped me process what had just happened. New Circle works in a cognitive way, it shakes people out of the moroseness of daily life. I created the possibility of having a boyfriend, something that incredibly had not occurred to me so far. This would have been late summer 2002 and I was due to meet my parents in Budapest, to

---

[9] friendlier

attend a series of concerts which included music composed by my mother. Paula was living there, married to an Austrian, and she showed us around. It was through her that I met Maarten, a Dutch journalist with a winning smile and beautiful eyes. During that summer in Budapest everything seemed possible. It was the beginning of the European trend of inner-city beaches, when shores of famous rivers would be covered in sand, deck chairs and cocktail bars playing bossa-nova and lazy drum'n'bass. Budapest was also full of secret bars. We would enter a boring look coffee shop and be led through a back door into another world of bohemian rhapsodies. And the actual old Hungarian coffee shops still partied like it was 1899 when you could bump into Bela Bartok having a *pastis* with the Secessionists. The rudeness of the waiters was legendary, but we could spend an entire day sat at a *fin-de-siècle* café having just one espresso and elicit no reaction from the staff.

The night I met Maarten I also met some European movers and shakers. I kept trying to follow their conversation in German, trying to resurrect the knowledge I acquired during 3 years at the Goethe Institut, but the thickness of their different accents made me give up. Besides, I could tell Maarten was paying special attention to my silk lilac dress and ready smile, and I sensed a whiff of romance in the air. He was one of those people with easy charisma, and everyone liked him. I only spent 4 days in Budapest, but we definitely had something going by the time I left. I think I was on my second Apple computer then, but remote communication was not so reliant on emails yet, and as for smart phones, I only had a trusty old Nokia. But I got postcards instead, which was nicer – and I still have most of them, probably due to nostalgia. I think I kept them over the years because it was evidence that I'd actually managed to keep a relationship going for at least a while. Maarten wanted to come see me in London, and I agreed, with a new species of butterflies in my tummy. I picked him up from Belsize Park tube in my old VOLVO and took him home. That night we started our fiery, passionate courtship. I couldn't believe I'd found someone like him, and he kept telling me the same. I should have remembered the story of Icarus…

I grew into my own person with Maarten, sexually and affectionately. There seemed to be no end to our happiness, even with a long-distance relationship. He was besotted to the point where he had to take one of my shirts back to Holland with him every time he left. At first, I relished the attention, because I'd been on a love draught of sorts. But then slowly and in a back-of-the-mind kind of way I began to think this kind of neediness was a bit over the top. But I loved being loved and so I ignored the whispers from my intuition. Maarten had told me about his ex, an Austrian girl he kept slandering every time he spoke of her (thankfully not often). I wasn't canny enough to even wonder if, in a twist of fate, it was me he'd be dissing next, if he ever moved on. But he once said to me that if we ever broke up it wouldn't be him to do it. I found that remark very odd but a welcome reassurance, even if I had asked for none. And so, we continued our long-distance relationship, with visits to London and Utrecht whenever we could steal some time. He wanted to meet my parents and we decided to plan a trip to Brazil.

Before we left, Maarten took me to his parents' house near Delft (where the blue tiles and Vermeer come from). It was a strange evening in December, before Christmas. His mother was defiant and his father meek, but both seemed a bit wary of him. I knew he had never had a good relationship with his mother, and I thought I could see why. I found myself talking out of my comfort zone, in German (they spoke no English), not allowing silences to linger too long because it became somewhat uncomfortable. The impression I had was that his parents were scared to do anything that frightened Maarten off. Before this meeting, he told me, he hadn't met or spoken to them for a couple of years and that I had been the reason for this reunion. I was flattered but the weight of this responsibility was a bit much. But we set off to Brazil, where at first all was perfect, because we stayed at my mother's office (my old home). We left for the beach house a few days later, for Christmas and New Year's Eve.

This was when Maarten's super sensitivity started to flare up. Firstly, he couldn't stay at the beach longer than beyond 9am because of mosquitoes. Then he started to get irritated by the sound of my father's slippers. Then there were a series of mishaps; on New Year's Eve we were having sex, but the phone kept ringing and I knew it was my dad, calling from the party we were meant to be at. I had to answer the phone in case my dad came back, which annoyed Maarten. The next day we had some food at a seaside Japanese restaurant, but on the way back to the car I spotted a cloud of massive wasps buzzing towards him. Paranoid that a sting would flare up his skin allergy, I shoved him into the car, and he bumped his head. He was furious and spent half the journey back not talking to me. A few days later we all went to Cunha, the old colonial town in Rio state. He insisted on taking my parents to the best, most expensive restaurant available, but they said they were happy with the one they always went to. Maarten was angry at me for not pressuring them enough to accept.

These little incidents were piling up, and I was starting to see a side of him I wasn't crazy about. It is very possible he thought exactly the same thing about me. I think I even confided in my mum, wondering if he was the right person for me. I am sure we'd lost each other by then. I detected a change in his behaviour once we returned. He was colder, more distant. Being physically apart helped the estrangement. I could sense what was coming but desperately tried to avoid it. Why? I felt we weren't suited and yet I was still in love with him. In the end he dumped me on the phone from Holland, and I was heartbroken. It took me a good year and a half to get over it. I was still trying to communicate with him afterwards, as if I was the bailiff for an unpaid debt: the words he once said about never being the one who breaks up. I couldn't believe someone I loved could act so dishonourably. But as time went by, I started to wonder why he had said those words, because deep down, I knew they were a fiction. No one can promise a thing like that. Maybe I invited it by thought or deed. Recognizing that actually gave me a lot of freedom. True, I couldn't help thinking of either punching him or tipping a pint of beer on his head for at least 4 years after the break up. But I relaxed a bit about my rage and stopped trying to suppress it. He sent me a box of the stuff I left in Holland, and I returned the favour. I didn't hear anything from him for a long time, until Paula met him socially and told me he'd been dissing me to our mutual friends. I think I saw red and was ready to retaliate, but then I remembered him badmouthing his ex, early in our relationship. We had come full circle. I couldn't see it at the time, but eventually I realised this behaviour had more to do with him than me.

So here I was, thinking I had attained something solid in my hands, only to see it melt away through my fingers. I decided I needed a kick up the ass. I registered for New Circle's toughest course, Circle of Truth, or COT for a shortcut. I was so lost in my own grief that I didn't realise I was training to become an introduction leader for the First Circle. By the time I noticed where we were going, I considered dropping out because that goal was far from what I wanted. But I could see some value in sharpening my tools for standing in front of an audience, so I stayed on and completed the course. I didn't pass, but the amazing thing about it was the process I went through to learn the leader's manual. It was more like a book of spells. Learning and delivering each chapter meant having to overcome any fear or feeling of inadequacy or people looking at me. I had to be totally present with them, without judgement. I found out I wasn't nearly as compassionate as I thought. It was tough training, but it kept me distracted from the heartbreak.

I also had a spectacular comeback into the world of the living in the present when my application for funding got approved by a local authority film fund. I had to fight off 600 people on the first round, and 10 people on the second round. The last round involved convincing (or enrolling & registering, as we used to say at New Circle) the panel that my project was worthy of funding. I was really prepared: storyboards done with dolls, and I even brought my stereo with the music I wanted to use in it. Only later, when I'd won the funding, did it occur to me that I'd used my COT training to deliver my message without letting my nervousness get in the way. I was ecstatic, even if it wasn't that much money. I had a good team behind me, and we made a short film that looked like it cost ten times the money we spent. It went to many top festivals and won us some nominations and awards. I'll never forget the time it was screened at the National Film Theatre in London, as part of a female film festival. It was a packed cinema and I could barely hear the opening music to my own film because the beating of my heart was so loud it was like a sound system in my chest. At the after party I felt someone poking me and turned to find a big star raving to me about my film. I'd lost my film directing virginity.

By then I'd decided to leave the flat I shared with G & M. I thought, fuck it, I just can't live in the same place as these two anymore. It was a bit of a shame that it came to that because we did have some fun. I took lots of pictures for their band publicity which still get used on their gigs. I met them a couple of times after that, but I guess the part of me that's always trying to be nice and liked didn't want to rock the boat. I sent them a gift when their son was born, and invited them to my wedding, but they never replied. Who was I trying to fool? I just didn't want them in my life anymore – and I'd wager on the same feeling from them. How long does it take us to say no to circumstances we're no longer happy with? It took me quite some time to eliminate everything and everyone I no longer wanted around me, purely for compassionate or procrastination reasons. That's the gift of getting older, life becomes a bullshit-free zone.

My friend Hannah asked if I wanted to stay in her flat for a while. I said yes and moved out pretty quickly, with no bad feelings about it, at least on the surface. I was angry at being the one who had to leave the flat, but anger would take me nowhere, so I concentrated on my new home. It was an attic one bedroom flat, so perfect for my desire to finally have my own space. Hannah was around for a while with her baby son, but she left for Norway a few months later. This was a housing co-op flat, and I could not make a song and dance about being there as sub-letting was not allowed. But I felt a sense of relief I had not felt for many years. Not having to put up with behaviour I disagreed with or having to wait to use the bathroom. The big house we'd shared was in the same area, so I knew it fairly well, and loved it. I'd had my share of short doomed romances by then and decided to have a break, or the decision was made for me. I got a job on an American film shooting in Prague, so I set off for a month's filming at the last minute, replacing a Czech script supervisor who'd been fired…I was a bit jittery on my first day because in film circles it is known that Americans love firing people. I wondered if I'd be next, given that I'd had no time to prep anything.

It was a medium size film, which in American terms means around $11 million budget. I was given a 2-bed flat in the centre of the old town and ferried to work the same day I arrived. The director, who'd had a sleeper hit years before, was relieved to see me at least. His star was a big action hero, playing the lead on a film about the mob. I was thrown into this alien environment, trying to catch up as fast as I could. On my first few days on set I was really impressed with how the director choreographed his shots. He'd storyboarded the entire film, a sort of discipline I'd never come across before. I learned a lot watching him direct, but there was no doubt this was a macho testosterone set. A lot of bravado and swearing flying around. I got friendly with the British camera crew, because they had a similar sensitivity to mine. The camera operator, a Scot called Robert, had a confrontation with the director once because he had to shoot a sequence in which the lead character barges past a woman holding a young kid who was clearly terrorized by the whole thing. It was a long Steadicam shot, which means a full sequence done in one go, the camera attached to the camera operator's body, like an exoskeleton. Robert refused to go beyond take 4 because the child was very upset by now. I wondered what I'd do if it was me directing this film. It wasn't a subject I found fascinating and I probably wouldn't ever be in this situation. But if I had been, there were ways this unpleasantness could have been negotiated better.

I finished the film and got embroiled in some semi romances which certainly baffled me. An Estonian guy I'd met and flirted with at one of my mother's concert tours in Italy heard I was working in Prague and travelled by bus from the Baltics via Poland to visit me. Once there I did not have much time to spend with him, but on days off we did hang out. He was staying at my flat. Perfect opportunity for some last minute unscheduled few-night stands, but somehow it wasn't happening. I wondered what had made him cross 2 former soviet republics to join me. I confronted him. His answer was neither here nor there. But it became clear that a short – or long - affair wasn't his intention. So, he came and went without me ever finding out what he was after. Then I started to notice a handsome Czech camera driver outrageously flirting with me. And with a few other girls in the crew, I later found out. I was getting a bit fed up of the signals European men seemed to send out, only to take flight once there was a response to them. In this area I missed the way Brazilian men dated because it was always very clear what the procedure was. Here, I was flying blind. There was Irish Frank with his melting stares and instant departures, and Malcolm, who even met my parents in London once, but failed to meet my gaze when it mattered most. I was ready to throw the towel. It just seemed like hard work that never paid off. Although I did manage to have an extended snogging session with Jirko, a Czech man I'd met at a bar in the old Castle district of Cesky Krumlov. My friend Jana had already retired to our hostel, and I made my way back there eventually, lip-entangled with Jirko as in a crazy slow waltz through the cobbled medieval streets under pouring rain. He was a gentleman though, and we said our goodbyes through a gap in the door, like a scene from a film never shot.

I had been flirting with the idea of doing some music again, and all these mentally unavailable men were a great incentive to throw me right in the middle of playing again, not least because they provided plenty of material for torch song lyrics. My friend Chiara's ex-boyfriend Anders was now living in Mallorca with his brother, where they had a farm/ recording studio. He invited me for a long weekend of work and play, and I accepted straight away. I can't remember why or how, but Yara, who I hadn't seen in ages, hustled her way into the holiday as well, joining me on a cheap flight to the Balearic Islands on a warm April morning. Getting there, she seemed to complain about everything, but at least she had a good sense of humour. Besides, she was cheeky to the point of embarrassment, but fortunately our host found that quite funny. She was an outrageous flirt as well, although his statuesque Swedish girlfriend didn't seem to mind it one bit. Northern European social contracts, it seemed, were much more relaxed. Our long holiday consisted of partying until late, then start work at around 12 noon. I seemed to be the only one getting up earlier, at 9am. The weather was sunny but still fresh, and I'd stroll down to a grove behind the house were the trees were heavy with peaches and nectarines. I'd have breakfast on my own, writing lyrics with just birdsong for inspiration. That's how Tom Jobim [10] used to write, so I reckoned I was in good company. People would start emerging slowly, we'd have a late lunch and go to the studio afterwards. I recorded about 3 songs with Anders, two of which I wrote lyrics for. They were released on his label as part of 2 compilations. I was quite proud of myself.

Back in London and a few months later, my friend and old bandmate Charlotte invited me for Christmas in Amsterdam that year. She'd moved there recently, and I'd been to see her and other friends a few times since my job on the Dutch movie. I'd had one good experience with a Dutch man after Maarten, which had made my antennae turn across the English Channel towards the continent for once. This was after I'd had an affair with a gaffer on a job, one of the last times I messed around with a married man. This time I'd learned my lesson and made sure I never poked on another's territory again...

Charlotte had a friend called Jasper, a musician, and we got on really well. He invited me for dinner, and I thought there was no mistaking the

---

[10] Brazilian composer of *The Girl From Ipanema*

signals this time, but I was wrong. When he laid out a single mattress on the living room, I realised I still hadn't got the memo. I was upset at myself for not moving on from the same perceptions. 'When will I wake up?' I thought. I remembered that old Culture Club song, 'Mistake nº3', wondering which number I was at, presently. I couldn't sleep anyway. I wondered how much longer I could either fail to see the obvious or carry on attracting men who lived in a fog of their own. I got up very early, folded sheets and left Jasper a curt 'thank you for dinner' note. I hoped it was short enough for him to realise something was off. I walked along the quiet Amsterdam streets, my mind more upset than my heart, as the early morning sun shining off the dark canals guided my steps. I didn't see Jasper again and left the next day.

Weeks later I got an email from him asking if I was ok and that he expected me to stay for breakfast that day. I sent him an honest reply and I got a very candid email from him. I couldn't see it at the time, but we all have our own shit to rifle through, it seems. When we are hurt, we become self-centred, but it often has nothing to do with us. With Jasper it was the same. Yes, he did notice I had feelings for him and maybe he was naïve to invite me for dinner solo, but I also learned there is something transparent, like glass, about Northern European social habits. Very different from South American dating hierarchies. Jasper valued friendship more than love affairs and considered himself 'complicated' in matters of the heart… If I'd lived in Amsterdam and we'd become firm friends maybe it could have developed into something, but it was not to be. One year later I was back in Amsterdam for Christmas again, and had met Geert at a club party. We started dating pretty quickly and I thought I'd finally broken this dysfunctional spell. I saw Jasper again at Charlotte's house, and I could see the shock in his face when he realised Geert and I were going out. Clearly, our timing could not have been worse. I dated Geert for a year, it was a bit up and down and not how I thought it would go. But he took me to Helsinki for a short weekend where I saw the beauty of a totally frozen lake (I could stand on the solid water shore) and did some target shooting with Kalashnikovs and Colts, under an old Soviet-era bunker.

Around that time, I received the news that Jasper had taken his own life. I thought there was clearly some mistake, but no. I heard that he'd been depressed because his father had been diagnosed with Alzheimer's, and he'd started having therapy. He hanged himself not long after he started taking medication. I'll never know for sure, but I think it was too much for his brain chemistry. Because he was fine, healthy, happy and successful a couple of months before that. It was hard to accept that such a special person could have had such a fate.

I was hanging out with Charlotte quite often and felt closer to Holland than the UK at that point. I started to entertain the idea of leaving London. I'd met another Dutch guy that year, but when I invited him to a romantic dinner, he turned up with his best friend. Which must have been when I gave up on Dutch men. Although I still thought it might be some sort of weird sign that my time in England was coming to an end. It was like trying to make something work and failing miserably. I'd had to leave Hannah's flat – and in that process we also fell out for a couple of years. I'd been in London for, what, a bit over 10 years, and hadn't been able to build a solid base or even relationship? It's funny how I can now see I didn't want to be tied down to anything, and so I got exactly what I wanted – no ties and no security either. I'd had to find last-minute lodgings at a house owned by Tom, a Canadian lawyer who loved the sound of his own voice. It was one of those situations I thought I'd left behind ages ago: a house share with a couple of other guys I didn't know or care to know. We only had access to the kitchen and bathroom, as the front room was exclusively for Tom's use. I had a really small room at the back, all my stuff was in storage, and I remember crying me a river when I found myself there, back from an Amsterdam weekend, wondering what the hell I was doing with my life. Like Alice in Wonderland, I realised how pathetic too much crying can be once I noticed my suitcase was almost entirely wet with tears.

But the creative juices were flowing, at least. I was getting ready to shoot my second short film, financed by a wealthy investor who'd seen my first short and offered to pay for the new one. I got my cinematographer Bob to shoot it, and we filmed it one cold November night, inside a double decker bus which kept going around a one-way system in Croydon, South London. I was thinking how to get the edit of the film going and start organizing my move to Amsterdam. I had even found myself a little apartment in a nice central area, for €600 monthly rent, which was what a room cost in London. I hadn't quite organised myself for such a big move yet. Truth be told, I was a little weary of what a new life in Holland would be like. I quite liked my car but would obviously need to ditch it in a cyclist-dominated society.

But before I could think about it any further, I had to attend Bob's wedding in the first week of December. He had planned quite a celebration: beautiful church wedding, followed by a reception at the late Georgian Reform Club (founded in the last year of George IV's reign). We were meant to be ferried there by privately hired double decker Routemaster buses, but I decided to drive. At the entrance of the church I was given a leaflet by a red- haired chap dressed in black, who I assumed to be the priest. But he wasn't. I saw him later, at the reception, when he joined our small group in a corner. My producer Chloe greeted him, but I didn't know him. I felt his beady eyes on me throughout the conversation, but he seemed to gravitate between various groups of people, like an over-social grasshopper. During the meal I realised I knew this guy. He was referred to as 'Red' by Bob and Chloe, presumably because of his more socialist sympathies – whereas Bob was a Conservative through and through. I had actually met him years before at one of Bob's famous barbecue parties. I remembered him looking very pink and stressed, wearing a tatty green jumper and carrying some foliage around the garden. His name was Jack, and throughout that whole evening we kept gravitating towards each other like a slightly out of synch dance. Bob had pulled all the stops to make his wedding fabulous. After dinner there was cheese and cognac, classy DJ, cigars and top wines flowing all night. Towards the end of the party I found myself sat on a table with Jack and another half-asleep guest, both worse for wear. It was 2am and I was a bit tired, wanting to go home. Jack didn't look like he was going to ask for my number, so I stuck my card in his pocket and left. I thought this might seem a bit forward, but I reckoned he looked so wasted he wouldn't know how the card had got there the next day. I don't think he noticed me leaving. I got onto one of Soho's over-priced rickshaws and wondered if I'd hear back from him.

I got a text message 2 days later saying, 'we bonded and should get together again'. We had our first date a week later, just a meal and some drinks in Central London. At a certain point the conversation got a bit heavy, because he'd just lost a sister to cancer. I remember my first impressions of Jack as someone who spoke for ages, but never staying on the same subject. That night he did a bit of that, but he seemed depressed, which was to be expected. I wasn't entirely sure he was attracted to me and thought maybe it was just meant to be a friendship after all. We parted in a subdued way, neither being too sure of what was happening. He asked me out again, and this time we had a long day together, going to a Greek restaurant for lunch, then taking a long walk across the Thames and somehow ending up at the Phoenix Arts centre bar in Charing Cross Road for dinner. This was pre-Christmas, and I hadn't realised there were some drag queens doing a show, dressed as Santa in red PVC. But the food was good, and we were actually synchronizing on the same vibe now. We started to date properly that night, and I invited him for dinner on Christmas day.

I had a sense of anticipation about our Christmas meal. Fortunately, the house was empty, Tom had gone to the Far East and his other lodger, a fat Swede with a bad case of BO, whose room was right next to mine, had also left for the holidays. When I'd first moved in, he tried to be friendly, but I couldn't get over the fact that he had the charisma of a John Christie[11]. I had to go past the door to his room and there was always a sort of invisible cloud of uncleanliness and stale chips, his dinner almost every night. There was another lodger, a Chinese guy who never left his room. And Tom had a ginger cat which meowed on a very deep sound register. Its poo stank the entire house. Luckily the cat was nowhere to be seen on the day I picked Jack up from Liverpool Street station. I had made roast beef and trimmings. The meat was hard as a rock and the meal was beyond poor, but we were more interested in each other. We spent the entire weekend together, watching old movies and getting to know each other on a deeper level. What I remember from our first few days together was a sense of ease and familiarity. I felt I could be fully myself with Jack. I didn't think I'd felt this way with any other man in my past.

Not long after we started going out, I met his family in Southampton. He was one of 10 brothers and sisters, and there was also a huge number of nephews and nieces. His mum had died years before, but I met his father, who was almost 85 years old. We drove down from London, trying to balance the beer cake I had baked for his birthday party. Any family gathering with this lot was like going to a big party because there were so many of them! Sometimes it was a bit overwhelming to be chatting

---

[11] Infamous 1950s British serial killer.

with so many different people at the same time, but I got used to it. They welcomed me into the family fold with grace and a big heart. As time went by, I got to know each of them better, especially Jack's dad. After so many years of bad timings and ships passing in the night scenarios, I felt a stillness which was deliciously new to me and endures to this day.

Afterword

I feel like I have nothing else to say about my past life at this point. I met Jack 12 years ago, and 6 years ago we got married, twice in the UK (registry and party) and once in Brazil, for my parents and friends.

I had finally met Jack because I stopped looking for a partner. I figured I could be happy on my own anyway, and then he came along. In 2012 I shot my third film, a medium length fantasy story set in a school for special needs children. With this film, I was absolutely certain I could cast a famous actor in it, even if everyone else doubted it. But he came in, for 2 hours, graciously giving me a chunk of his Sunday. Because I asked him to. I put everything on hold for his availability. Because I believed he would say yes to us. This film came to me out of nowhere, when I wasn't thinking about it, or at least not desperately wanting it. I found out that thinking about something with a burning desire is different from desperately wanting it. There is no way to conceal the vibration of lack which exists in the word 'want'.

The past few years I have been immersed in writing books and screenplays, planning my next films, and doing all sorts of personal development study. I did some more New Circle courses, which really provided the cognitive structure for flying higher and dipping my toes in the unknown. Then I continued reading philosophy, religion, and what is now called self-help, by which I mean books to raise awareness. I came across all sorts, all of which I highly recommend: Joe Dispenza, Napoleon Hill, Emerson, Hegel, Bob Proctor, James Allen, Esther Hicks, even the Bible had a different taste.

This book came out of my first connection with this blackness. So dear reader, whoever you are, I thank you for reading my book and joining my journey into the past. Writing it has been like sinking 20,000 leagues under the sea, or a voyage to the centre of the earthly mysteries of what I've been doing my whole life.

As I dive deeper into it, I feel courageous enough to put my creations out there in the world, in the faith that it inspires, dazzles or serves people in some way. And who knows, maybe I'll gather enough material for a Volume II…

Luciana Colleoni
London, November 2018

Printed in the United States
By Bookmasters